# 7 Divine Laws

To Awaken Your

# Best Self

# 7 Divine Laws

## To Awaken Your

# Best Self

SWAMI MUKUNDANANDA

HarperCollins *Publishers* India

First published in India in 2021 by
HarperCollins *Publishers*

Building 10, Tower A, 4th Floor, DLF Cyber City, Phase II,
Gurugram Haryana – 122002, India
www.harpercollins.co.in

2 4 6 8 10 9 7 5 3 1



P-ISBN: 978-93-9032-708-9
E-ISBN: 978-93-9032-709-6



Typeset in 11.5/15.8 Minion Pro at
Manipal Technologies Limited, Manipal

Printed and bound at
MicroPrints India, New Delhi

*This book is dedicated to my beloved Spiritual Master, Jagadguru Shree Kripaluji Maharaj, who illuminated the world with the purest rays of divine knowledge and sweetened it with the goodness of divine love. He taught me, by his example, the importance of nurturing souls with love and care to help them realize a glorious future. He reminded humankind about the supreme process of building a noble value system through selfless and ceaseless devotion to God. I am confident that by his blessings this book will help to inspire and elevate seekers, thereby creating a better world.*

# Contents

# Introduction

WE ALL wish to be better. The desire to awaken our best self is as natural to us as heat is to fire. No matter how good we may be, a feeling remains, 'I must improve further. I am not yet the ideal version of myself.'

The same yearning for growth manifests in our works as well. Despite what we may have accomplished in life, an inner voice says, 'I am yet not satisfied; I wish to do even better. I desire to be a better parent/child; a better husband/wife; a better boss/employee; a better teacher/student.' The list is endless…

What is the source of this aspiration, and why is it such an integral part of us? Well, the yearning to grow comes from the Creator Himself. The Bhagavad Gita states:

*mamaivānśho jīva-loke jīva-bhūtaḥ sanātanaḥ* (15.7)

'All living beings in the world are eternal fragmental parts of the Supreme.'

By nature, each part is spontaneously attracted to its source. Since our source is God—and He is perfect—we too seek to be more godlike. That is just the way we have been made. Our soul is destined for perfection, and hence, it keeps prodding us to progress further.

## The Evolution of the Soul

Around us, we witness Nature incubating the evolution of carbon—in the earth's crust—into diamond, over billions of years. In a shorter timeframe, mud evolves to grass, which is grazed by cows and transformed into milk. The milk gets converted to curds from which butter is extracted. And butter finally evolves to ghee, which gets offered on the sacred altar as a symbol of purity.

However, the creation of material products, like ghee and diamonds, is not the primary purpose of the grand scheme of the Universe. Rather, Nature's chief objective is to nurture the evolution of all souls to super-consciousness over a continuum of lifetimes. And until we fulfil that divine plan, we cannot be content.

The American philosopher Ralph Waldo Emerson expressed this very brilliantly in his essay 'The Over-Soul':

> *We grant that human life is mean. But how did we find out that it is mean? What is the ground of this old discontent? What is this universal sense of want and ignorance, but the fine innuendo by which the soul makes its enormous claim?*

The nudging of our soul that Emerson refers to was scripted in us by our Creator, to ensure we keep striving ever forward. It will only quieten when we manifest the infinite potential latent in us.

Dear Reader, you have also experienced this nudging of your soul for progress, and that is why you have chosen to read this book 'to awaken your best self'.

## The Dilemma We Face

The problem is not that we do not want perfection. The problem is that we strive for it year after year, but do not achieve success. This is our predicament. We aspire to reach the stars but find ourselves glued to our lower instincts. We have our head in the sky but our feet on the earth.

Why are personal growth and life transformation so difficult? Does Creation wish us to fail? Of course not! The purpose behind the Universe's grand design is to make us succeed. Our own unawareness of the laws of the Universe creates the impediment. Growth and accomplishment are the fruits of knowledge, not ignorance.

The *Adhyātma Rāmāyan* explains:

*ajñānamevāsya hi mūlakāraṇam* (Uttar Kand 5.9)

'Nescience is the root cause of all stagnation.' Consider the following hilarious example:

*I once saw a billboard advertisement picturing a snarling dog and a smug cat. The dog had the most ferocious expression on its face and was trying to pounce on the cat. Yet, just a whisker away, the feline sat blissfully unperturbed and even amused.*

*The caption of the advertisement read: The Power of Knowledge!*

*The dog was leashed; it could only bark and growl within the periphery of its tether. And the cat was aware of the simple fact: 'The dog does not have the power to breach its leash. If I stay outside its circle, I am safe.'*

Knowledge of the 'Law of the Leash' had bestowed freedom and peace of mind to the cat. If such a trivial piece of knowledge could make such a big difference, then what might be said of the benefits of knowing the laws of the Universe?

The purpose of this book is to acquaint you with the laws governing your life and how you can align your existence with them. Over the last three decades, I have taught these principles to millions and seen the difference this knowledge has made to their lives. I have no doubt it will benefit you as well.

## The Divine Laws

We all know that water boils at 100 degrees centigrade. So, we are not surprised to see it remain liquid at ninety-five degrees centigrade. Nor are we astonished to see it evaporate on reaching boiling point, for this conforms to the physical laws of the universe. These laws of nature govern the phenomena of electricity, magnetism, gravity, health, light, and the like.

We humans too create laws for the regulation of society. These man-made laws get instituted one day and can be repealed in future. However, Nature's laws are different. They are eternally valid irrespective of time, place, and circumstance. For example, whether we jump off the Qutub Minar or the Eiffel Tower, in both places the law of gravity will bring us down with a thud. It matters little whether we are aware of the law and agree with it or not.

Like the laws regulating physical phenomena, there are also spiritual principles governing the journey of life. Knowledge of them helps us understand why success comes so easily to some but remains a struggle for others; why some are still putting on their shoes, while others have finished the race. The beauty is that like the physical laws of nature, the divine principles governing success and fulfilment in life are also valid forever.

In this book, we shall discuss the seven most important divine laws of life. These precepts, which govern human existence, have been gleaned from the Vedic scriptures:

1. The Law of Infinite Potential
2. The Law of Incremental Growth
3. The Law of Beliefs
4. The Law of Happiness
5. The Law of Sublimation
6. The Law of Love
7. The Law of Mentorship

What are these laws? How can our life be enriched by their knowledge and application?

I sincerely believe you are as eager to know the answers as I am keen to explain them. So, without further ado, let's proceed—one page at a time—on a joyous journey through the seven chapters of this book.

# 1

# The Law of Infinite Potential

## The Making of a Genius

*Mensa is an international society for the super-intelligent. Admission to it is granted only to those who achieve a percentile score of ninety-eight or above on standard intelligence quotient (IQ) tests. The society has almost 150,000 members from over a hundred countries.*

*Yet, in 1954, eight years after its inception, Mensa's worldwide membership had dwindled to four. The person who lifted the organization to its present glory was Victor Serebriakoff from Austria. He took over its presidency when it was down in the dumps, and held it for nearly twenty long years, until his death in 2000.*

*Intriguingly, during Serebriakoff's childhood, nobody would have ever guessed the glorious achievements that lay ahead for him. He was born in penury in a slum colony. When he was fifteen years old, his schoolteacher declared to him, 'Victor, you are a dunce. You will never amount to anything in life.'*

*Convinced of his stupidity, Victor dropped out of school. For the next seventeen years, he engaged in menial works. Later, while working as a lumberjack, he happened to apply for a job in the army. As a part of the selection process, they tested his IQ. The test was designed to gauge IQ to a maximum of 161. His score went beyond the scale, which meant he was a genius.*

*That one piece of knowledge transformed his life. He began working hard to educate himself in his vocation. He became an expert in lumberjack technology, and where previously he had only performed menial tasks, he now wrote books on the trade. He also researched the topic of Intelligence Quotient, and became an expert, writing widely popular books on it.*

What was the eureka moment in Serebriakoff's life? It happened when he discovered he was not a dunce but a genius. Can there be such a eureka moment in our life as well? Sure, if only we correct one little blunder.

## The Mistake We Make

Like Victor Serebriakoff, we too are held back by our false beliefs. Our mistake is to think of the material body as the self. But the body is merely a bag of flesh and bones; identification with it cripples the belief in our potential. Instead, if we could realize our nature as divine souls, our consciousness would become unfettered from matter. We would then come in touch with infinite possibilities for personal growth.

Hence, the first point taught in the Bhagavad Gita is knowledge of the self:

*antavanta ime dehā nityasyoktāḥ śharīriṇaḥ*
*anāśhino 'prameyasya tasmād yudhyasva bhārata* (2.18)

'O scion of Bharat! The material body is perishable, but the soul is indestructible, immeasurable, and eternal. Therefore, rejecting all enfeebling thoughts, perform your duty.'

Sri Ramana Maharshi, a great sage who lived a hundred years ago, was renowned for emphasizing knowledge of the self in his teachings. When devotees came to him with problems and entreated him for blessings, he would respond: 'Think, **who is having these problems**. If you can discover your true nature, you will become unaffected.'

A devotee once said to him, 'Gurudev, I have so many problems. What should I do? And do not tell me to think, "**Who is having these problems**?"'

Ramana Maharshi responded, 'Think, who is it who is saying, "Do not ask me to think, **Who is having these problems?**"'

Ramana Maharshi's message was clear—we must first seek to understand ourselves. Without knowledge of our superior spiritual nature, we will remain tied to the trivial and mundane.

In our present bodily consciousness, our situation is like the eagle in the story below.

*An eagle's egg was placed amid a brood of chickens. Thinking it to be one of their own, the hens lovingly hatched it along with their own eggs. Consequently, the baby eagle which emerged from it grew up in the company of little chicks.*

*The result was 'monkey see, monkey do'. The chicks would say, 'Cluck, cluck, cluck', and the baby eagle would also cackle along. The chicks would flutter their wings and hop clumsily on the ground. The eagle would do the same, unaware of its God-given ability to fly at altitudes of 10,000 feet above the ground.*

*One day, an adult eagle flew by. The baby eagle looked at it with amazement, and exclaimed, 'Wow, what a majestic bird! How is it flying at such a glorious height with so much elegance?'*

*'That is an eagle', replied the chickens. 'It is the king of birds; naturally, its abilities are far greater. We cannot do what it can do.'*

*The baby eagle believed the chickens' sermon, and it continued its pathetic life, fluttering and cackling like them. What a pity! It was born to rule the skies but had become conditioned to flutter on the ground.*

Like the eagle, we too were fashioned to sparkle in the magnificence of our spirit but became illusioned to wallow in the mediocrity of bodily conceptions. As a poet said: *phūla chunane āye the bāge-hayāt meṅ, khāra jhāra meṅ dāmana ulaphā kara raha gaye* 'We had come to pluck flowers from the garden of life, but in the ensuing hustle and bustle of human existence, we ended up entangled in thorns.'

On realizing our soul nature, what becomes our potential? The next section provides the answer.

## The Glorious Destiny of Our Soul

The soul's splendour comes from the fact that it is a tiny part of God. The *Vedānt Darshan* states: *anśho nānā vyapadeśhāt* (2.3.43) 'All souls are eternal fragmental parts of the Divine.' In other words, we too are divine, like God Himself.

Consider the example of a huge fire and a tiny spark. The fire can incinerate an entire forest and consign it to flames. In comparison, a tiny spark is only miniscule. Yet, the spark too has the capacity to ignite an entire forest. **Likewise, as fragments of the Supreme Divine Personality, we have immense potential inherent in our soul.**

Now, listen to a second cause—which is even more powerful—for the splendid future that awaits us. The reason is that God Himself wishes to share His magnificence with us. In the Vedas, a word for Him is Brahman. Jagadguru Shree Kripaluji Maharaj explains the meaning of Brahman:

*brahma vṛihatvāt asa baṛā, jāko ādi na anta*
*baṛā bṛinhaṇatvāt asa, aurana kare ananta*
(*Bhakti Śhatak* verse 51)

This verse states that the definition of Brahman has two parts to it:

1. Brahman is He who is infinitely big. This is evident because God holds innumerable universes within His being.
2. Brahman is He who makes others big. This second definition of God is of great relevance to us. It implies that **the Lord desires His little parts to grow in divine virtues and become perfect like Himself.**

Therefore, to want to awaken your best self is not an egotistical craving, rather, it is what God desires from us. In fact, it is a mistake to think, 'I will always remain a sinner and can do nothing about it.' Swami Vivekananda expressed this so aptly:

*These Prophets were not unique; they were men as you and I. They had attained super-consciousness, and you and I can do the same. The very fact that one person attained that state indicates that all men can do so. And that ultimately is religion.*

Naturally, we revere saints of the past like Soordas, Tulsidas, Meerabai, Tukaram, Guru Nanak, Kabir, and Narsi Mehta. But merely putting them on an altar and worshipping them is not our goal. Rather, we too must strive to become like them—transcendental in virtues and qualities—for that is true spirituality.

The same idea is mentioned in the Bible as well: 'Be perfect, therefore, as your heavenly Father is perfect.' (Matthew 5:48)

With the help of these examples, scriptural quotations, and logic, we can now understand the first of the seven divine laws:

---

## The Law of Infinite Potential

*All souls have infinite potential for growth, whatever be their present state.*

---

In this statement, the word 'potential' is especially important. It kindles hope and makes us optimistic about the future, encouraging us to plan for grand accomplishments. This positivity is further amplified by the word 'infinite', implying our scope for growth is without limit.

Equipped with the knowledge of this law, we can cultivate the growth mindset. What is that? Let us learn about it in the next section.

## Fixed vs Growth Mindset

Many people are of the 'fixed mindset'. They believe their skills are determined by destiny or circumstance and cannot be developed any further. Thus, they do not toil to enhance their competencies. 'When progress is decided by fate, why should we try?' Thinking along these lines, they remain stuck in mediocrity all their life. In this way, they squander away their immense human potential.

The biggest calamity is not the waste of natural resources. **The biggest calamity in the world is the waste of human resources—the untapped capacity of people with the 'fixed mindset'.** Consequently, the biggest global progress would happen if such people could change their attitude to the 'growth mindset'.

What is the 'growth mindset'? Here is a wonderful example of this beautiful perspective to make it come alive.

*Pablo Casals was a world-famous cellist from Spain. He lived till the ripe age of ninety-five and continued practising his music until the end.*

*In his final year, a reporter asked, 'Mr Casals, you are ninety-five years old and the greatest cellist who has ever lived. Why do you still practise six hours a day?'*

*Pablo Casals' answer was stupendous: 'Because I think I am making progress.'*

This is the 'growth mindset'. People like Mr Casals excel in life because they do not take their talents as predetermined. They believe that with proper effort, there is unlimited scope for progress. Hence, they never take good enough to be enough. They constantly endeavour to stretch themselves towards ever-greater success.

At this point, I would like to clarify that success does not mean simply increasing the number of digits in your bank balance or the number of bedrooms in your house. **True success is the blossoming of our soul in who we are and what we do. To succeed in life is to become the best that we can become, and to do the best that we can do.** And to have faith that we can become like that is the progressive attitude.

*One of the finest architects in the modern world has been Frank Lloyd Wright. His creative period spanned seventy years, during which he designed more than 1,000 buildings. Amongst them are many world-renowned monuments, like the Guggenheim Museum in New York and Hollyhock House in Los Angeles.*

*If a journalist would ever ask him, 'Which of the numerous buildings you designed do you like the best?' he would always respond, 'My next one.'*

*Frank Lloyd Wright's answer revealed his growth mindset. Every time he designed a new building, his goal was to excel his previous best. He could easily have become complacent because he was already the best in the world in his profession. But his competition was not with others; it was with his own self. His passion was for stretching himself.*

We see from this example that **growth does not happen automatically. It ensues when we commit ourselves to excellence in our endeavours.** In the realm of spirituality, you see such commitment in the life of saints. They pursued enlightenment with steadfast resolve. They resolved to be more persistent than the difficulties. Ultimately their commitment to reach the highest standard of personal excellence paid dividends. For example, Dhruv (the son of King Uttānapād) was only a four-year-old when he began his quest for God. How did he succeed where millions failed?

The answer is quite simple. When he went into the forest to perform austerities, he simply kept increasing the intensity of his spiritual practice, until he attracted divine grace and attained the goal.

The same principle applies to other spheres of human activity. Thomas Watson Sr. was the legendary CEO of International Business Machines (IBM). His company policy was 'As of this second, quit doing less-than-excellent work.' With such a commitment to stretching himself and his subordinates, he steered IBM's growth, from 1914 to 1956, into an international corporate giant.

Lack of knowledge of the Law of Infinite Potential is the reason people develop defeatist mindsets, which is so unfortunate. They can be compared to the eagle, in our story earlier, which believed it was a chicken. Wasn't that pitiable? Well, even more pathetic is to see humans believe they cannot grow and thereby make lame excuses to rationalize their stagnation.

What are these excuses? The next section describes them.

## The Loser's Limp

*You may have witnessed this spectacle in cricket. The batsman strikes the ball hard, lifting it over the midfielder's head. Since the outfield is slow, the fielder thinks he has a chance of catching the ball before it crosses the boundary. He turns around and gives the ball a chase. But then at one point in the chase, he realizes that he will not be able to catch up with the ball.*

*Suddenly, the fielder slows down and begins limping, as if he has sprained his foot or twisted his leg. The spectators, say, 'Oh ... look at the poor fellow. He has hurt himself. No wonder he could not reach the ball.'*

This is called 'Loser's Limp', a rationalization for failing. Have you ever caught yourself or others using a loser's limp? Here are some typical ones along with my rejoinders to them.

**Loser's Limp:** 'I have not excelled in my profession because I am not a born engineer/doctor/lawyer, etc.'

**Rejoinder:** 'My dear friend, I have travelled to many countries. Everywhere I have heard of women giving birth to boys and girls. Never have I heard of mothers giving birth to engineers or doctors or lawyers. This implies that people are not born engineers/doctors/lawyers but get there by self-effort. If your condition for achieving success is to be born an expert, you are setting yourself up for failure.'

**Loser's Limp:** 'If only I could sing like her, I would definitely have succeeded.'

**Rejoinder:** 'Look, there is no point in speculating what you would have done if you had another's talents. The point of life is not to go shopping for others' abilities, but to make the best use of your own; and that is the only known way to develop more talent.'

**Loser's Limp:** 'The reason for my shortcomings is my parents. They made mistakes while raising me.'

**Rejoinder:** 'Maybe, but no one is perfect. Now think about this: if finger pointing is your habit, then no matter how conducive your external conditions, you will always remain in the same mess. People who succeed in the game of life are those who take responsibility for their life. They focus on solutions rather than problems, and as a result, become effective in what they do.

'Additionally, do not forget that the only way you will get better parents in your next birth is by focusing on doing your best in the present. That is the Law of Karma. You get in life what you deserve, not what you desire.'

**Loser's Limp:** 'I am not a born success. It is the reason for my poor show.'

**Rejoinder:** 'Listen, I come across many who say they are self-made men and women. But I never come across people who say they are self-made failures. Understand that nobody is born a success or failure. The keys to success are discipline and consistent effort. There is no substitute for hard work. Success means to anticipate obstacles on the way and knock them down instead of them knocking you down.'

These are only a sample of the thousands of Losers' Limps. We must resolve to immediately vanquish such alibis that keep us stuck in mediocrity and push ourselves to strive for excellence in our life and work. Let us take inspiration from the Vedic mantra:

*uttiṣhṭhata jāgrata prāpya varānnibodhata*

(*Kaṭhopaniṣhad* 1.3.14)

'Awake, arise, and stop not, till the goal is reached.'

To drive this pursuit for a successful life, we have an immensely powerful engine within us. Let us gain knowledge about it in the next section.

## The Hundred Horsepower Engine Inside Us

*Ramdas Majhi belonged to a tribal village in the state of Jharkhand in India. The poor inhabitants of his village subsisted on cotton farming, which was the only kind of agriculture possible in that dry terrain. Like all other villagers, Ramdas Majhi lived in a thatched mud hut. He was respected by everyone for his amicable nature, and in fact, was the village headman.*

*Once Ramdas Majhi went on a government-sponsored holiday trip to Kolkata. There he won a jackpot worth ten crore rupees. On returning to his village, his standard of living was transformed. Among other things, he built a triple-storied brick house for himself and purchased a Rolls-Royce car.*

*Now, in the evening he would drive through the village in his Rolls-Royce. The vehicle would move slowly. Sitting in it, Ramdas Majhi would often turn left and right to speak to people passing by. Being of amicable nature, he would even turn all the way around to greet people behind his car. Despite his inattentiveness to the road ahead, the Rolls-Royce never had an accident. Why?*

*The reason was that Ramdas Majhi never turned on the ignition switch to start the engine. He had two horses pulling the car in the manner of a horse-drawn cart. What a pity! The Rolls-Royce was fitted with a hundred horsepower engine. Unaware of what was under the car's bonnet, Ramdas Majhi was getting it pulled externally by two horses.*

The Rolls-Royce had a powerful engine under its bonnet that remained unused. Have you ever wondered what is inside your bonnet? An infinite power engine—a fragment of the Almighty Lord Himself. Imagine the power latent in your soul!

You may ask, 'How can we access the power of our inner engine? How can we go within ourselves to reach our soul?' The story below shows the way.

*One of the foremost painters and sculptors of modern India in the last century, Ramkinkar Baij, was a faculty member of Kala Bhavan, the fine arts department of Visva-Bharati University in Santiniketan, West Bengal. Visva-Bharati University was conceived and established by Rabindranath Tagore and is a globally acclaimed university for languages, literature, comparative literature, and fine arts.*

*Baij is credited with popularizing modern Indian sculpture. One day, he unveiled a stone statue of the Buddha that he had worked upon with great love.*

*Press reporters asked him the secret by which he made the statue so profound and 'Buddha-like'.*

*He responded, 'When I first looked at the stone block, I could see the Buddha in it. All I did was to remove what was not the Buddha.' It was so simple.*

In the same manner, if we wish to go within ourselves to reach our divine nature, we too will have to wean away fallacies that warp our perspective, values, and beliefs. These fallacies limit us in two ways. Firstly, they dupe us into the fixed mindset. But more importantly, they confuse us about the true meaning of success itself. Thus, **even if we do have the growth mindset, intellectual fallacies warp our definition of success. Therefore, we short-change ourselves and chase meaningless goals from morning till night**, like the dog in the story below.

*A dog lived as the pampered pet of the owner of a big bungalow. The hound loved to run in the lawn in front of the house. Every time a car went by, the dog would chase it, barking furiously till it reached the end of the lawn. Then it would wait for the next car to appear and chase it till the other end. In this way, it would chase scores of cars throughout the day.*

*The dog's behaviour was very amusing to the neighbour. One day, he asked the owner, 'I wonder if the dog actually catches any of the cars it chases?'*

*'That is not what I am worried about,' replied the mongrel's owner. 'I wonder what it will do if it ever manages to catch any car.'*

The dog had a futile goal—chasing cars without any purpose. We too must ponder whether the goals that we run after in life are in fact worthwhile or are they equally futile?

The Vedic scriptures call the fallacies that are causing our confusion as *viparyaya.* Maharshi Patanjali states:

*viparyayo mithyājñānam atadrūpa pratiṣhṭham*

(*Yoga Sutras* 1.8)

'*Viparyaya* is erroneous understanding of the self, which is not based on accurate knowledge.'

The Shreemad Bhagavatam details this concept of *viparyaya* further:

*anityānātmā duḥkheṣhu viparyaya matirhyaham*

(10.40.25)

Maharshi Ved Vyas states in this verse that under the influence of the material energy, maya, our intellect has suffered three misconceptions.

What are these fallacies that we believe to be true?

**The first intellectual misconception is the illusion that our material possessions will always remain with us.**

We forget the day shall come when we will leave behind everything we possess and continue to the life hereafter. The British poet, Thomas Gray, did not mince words while stating this truism in his poem, *Elegy Written in a Country Churchyard*:

*The boast of heraldry, the pomp of power,*
*And all that beauty, all that wealth ever gave,*
*Awaits alike the inevitable hour.*
*The paths of glory lead but to the grave.*

Let us learn this lesson from the Shreemad Bhagavatam.

*The famed renunciant monk, Avadhoot Dattatreya, once visited the palace of Raja Jeemutketu. Hailing the king, who was seated on his throne, Dattatreya exclaimed, 'O King! Can I spend the night in your dharmashala?'*

*'Mind your tongue, O Sage!' responded the indignant king. 'I have such an opulent palace, and you are declaring it a dharmashala?'*

*Then Dattatreya compassionately explained to the king why he used the term. 'Rajan, I first came by this place fifty years ago. At that time, you were not on the throne. There was a taller man with a large turban. He was probably your grandfather. That painting on the wall, by the left of your throne, I believe is of him.*

*'The second time I came here was twenty-five years ago. By then, your grandfather was no more. The monarch in his place was a man with big moustaches. I presume he was your father. That painting on the wall, on your right, seems to be of him.*

*'This time, your father is also not to be seen, and you are now king in his place. It appears people reside here for a little while, and then they are gone. That is why I called your palace a dharmashala.'*

The story highlights the temporary nature of our material possessions, which we mistakenly assume to be permanent. That is why Jagadguru Kripaluji Maharaj explains how a wise person should live:

*jaga meṅ raho aise govinda rādhey,*
*dharmaśhālā meṅ yātrī rahe jyoṅ batā de*

(*Radha Govind Geet*)

'Live in this world as travellers stay in hotels. They do not accord importance to aesthetics of their room, for they know they must vacate it next morning.'

However, in fallacious understanding, we mistake temporary things as permanent. Naturally, our value system and idea of true success is affected by it.

**The second intellectual misconception is that we look on our material body as the self.**

This fallacy is like a driver sitting in a Mercedes car, who on being asked his identity, responds, 'I am a Mercedes'. Will you not call such a driver an ignorant fool? He has mistaken the car for himself.

Our mistake is of an even larger magnitude. On being asked, 'Who are you?' we reply with our physical designations of nationality, caste, profession, relationships: 'I am an Indian/ American/Italian …', 'I am a Brahmin/Kshatriya …', 'I am a Marwari/Gujarati/Punjabi …', 'I am a Plant Superintendent/ professor/CEO …', 'I am the wife/daughter/sister of so and so', and so on. We confuse our bodily designation as ourselves.

Unfortunately, the confusion has been further strengthened by the presumptions of modern science. Although, individually, most scientists believe in the existence of the non-material soul, bizarrely, science as a body of knowledge makes no mention of it. Thus, we are left with the reductionist understanding that the 'self' is just a combination of atoms and molecules in the body and their mutual interaction.

The obvious question that arises is that if we are simply a combination of atoms and molecules, then what accounts for the free will we possess? In that case, we should be like computers that work according to their programming but cannot make independent free choices. However, even scientists realize they possess the freedom to choose. Can the reductionist understanding of the 'self' as the sum of the body's physical parts explain the source of our free will?

Again, if we are just a bunch of atoms and molecules, from where does consciousness originate? We all know that atoms and molecules do not possess consciousness. Albert Szent-Györgyi, a Hungarian biochemist and Nobel Prize winner in physiology, expressed this lacuna in the present scientific understanding: 'In my search for the basis of consciousness, I ended up with atoms and molecules. Somewhere along the line, life slipped out of my hands. Now in my old age, I am tracing my steps backward.'

He realized that insentient matter could not explain the phenomenon of life. However, if we ask material science the question, 'Who am I?' the answer we get is, 'You are the sum of the constituent parts of your body.'

This answer reminds me of *Frankenstein*, a novel by Mary Shelley. The doctor in the story gathered body parts from a graveyard. When he put them together, a living monster was created. The doctor had managed to make a living organism from insentient body parts. Think about it—science too claims that the 'self' is the mere outcome of the conglomeration of our physical parts!

The Vedas inform us that consciousness is not a product of the body's constituents; it is the symptom of the soul. Because of the soul's presence, there is life in the body; the moment it departs, the body becomes dead matter. Our identity of the 'self' comes not from dead matter but from the soul.

Suppose a king dreams of himself as a beggar. Unavoidably, he will suffer the woes of poverty till the dream continues, even though it is untrue. That is precisely our situation. Confusing ourselves with the material mind and body, we are identifying with the miseries that afflict it. The Ramayan states:

*moha niśhā saba sovanihārā,*
*dekhia sapana aneka prakārā*

As a person dreams while sleeping and loses contact with reality, we too are living an illusory existence in forgetfulness of ourselves. This is the second fallacy of our intellect.

**Our third intellectual misconception is the belief that in sensual pleasures, we can find the happiness that will satiate our soul.** We bear so much pain and misery chasing them, but do not realize our folly. Let us dwell on this point in greater depth.

Our five physical senses naturally hanker for their objects of gratification. We are convinced they will give us pleasure, and that is why we run after them. No doubt, sensual gratification does give a few moments of delight, and our desire gets quenched. However, the problem is that a little later the same desire we had fulfilled returns with redoubled intensity.

**If any desire, once gratified, remained permanently satiated, then fulfilling it would have resulted in happiness. But if the same desire keeps returning again and again, with even greater vigour, then its satiation is a misnomer.**

*lālā pānamivāṅguṣhṭe bālānāṁ stanya vibhramaḥ*

Sometimes, mothers put pacifiers in their baby's mouth to quieten them. Thinking it to be their mother's breast, the baby continues to suckle the nipple in the hope of getting milk from it. Grownups look at the baby's foolishness and laugh.

The fact is that our expectation of getting happiness by gratifying sensual desires is equally foolish. Such pleasure is ephemeral and is always accompanied by a variety of miseries, like attachment, anger, greed, and envy. It is like the fly which sat on honey to eat it but discovered that it could not get up. The honey had seemed like paradise to the fly but became its grave. Sensual delights are similar—pleasurable in the moment but painful in the long run.

The last few paragraphs may seem to be very philosophical, so let us take a humorous break.

*A man died and was taken to heaven. He found only decent people there, all engaged in decorous activities. He could not find one casino, night club, or movie theatre.*

*Feeling bored, the man asked God, 'Where are all the movie stars, politicians, pop musicians, and media celebrities?'*

*'They are all in hell,' replied the good Lord.*

*'In that case, hell must be a more interesting place. Heaven seems awfully unexciting in comparison. O God, can You please send me to hell for a day to check it out? If I like it, I will request a permanent transfer.'*

*'Sure, I can arrange for that,' replied the King of heaven. The next moment, the man was transported to hell.*

*On arriving in the nether abode, the man was pleasantly surprised. There were cool breezes blowing, and servants were ready to pamper him luxuriously. He was bathed in perfumed water and massaged in oil. He was attired in silk and fed a sumptuous feast. There was even an entertainment programme arranged for his viewing while he ate his food.*

*'Wow!' he thought. 'Heaven is insipid and lifeless. Hell is the place I want to be in.'*

*When his time was up, he was taken back to heaven. 'O Lord, thank You for all You have done for me. But hell is the place of parties and fun, and that is where I wish to be.'*

*'Not a problem,' replied the kind Lord. In a jiffy, the man was again transferred to hell.*

*However, this time the entire scenario had changed. The place was boiling hot like a cauldron. Devilish creatures with tridents were poking him all over. Cacophonous sound was splitting his ears, and the stench was like nothing he had ever smelled before. 'What is this place?' the man asked.*

*'This is hell,' responded the demons.*

*'But what was the place I was shown during my last visit?'*

*'That is only a model for visitors,' they said.*

Many factories have a visitor's model in their reception. It is not the real thing, only a replica. In this story, the visitor's model of hell was far different from the real thing. That is precisely the nature of sensual delights. We feel we will get great pleasure by savouring them, but the reality turns out to be much different.

This does not mean that every kind of desire is harmful. **Spiritual wisdom enables us to distinguish the advantageous desires from the unfavourable ones. Progress happens because of beneficial desires.** Examples of some beneficial desires are listed here:

- The desire to develop integrity and authenticity in our personality.
- The desire to make a positive impact in the lives of others around us.

- The desire to gain mastery over our mind and senses.
- The desire to create beautiful art, dance, or music for the pleasure of God.
- The desire to grow in humility and become free from conceit.
- The desire to detach the mind from painful entanglements.
- The desire to develop genuine selfless love.
- The desire to illumine our intellect with divine wisdom.

These are only a sample of the millions of possible uplifting desires we could nurture. **The spiritual perspective of life inspires us to cultivate such sublime and noble aspirations. On the other hand, the three intellectual fallacies, or *viparyaya,* all strengthen the materialistic viewpoint.** They make us believe that accumulating material objects for physical comfort is the supreme goal. Naturally, under this misconception, worthwhile progress is pushed aside, and we start chasing futile and meaningless goals.

By dispelling these fallacies of the intellect, we develop faith in the infinite potential of our soul. We establish beneficial and meaningful life goals. Then, our efforts align with the path of true progress.

All this discussion about growth gives rise to one doubt. Will not the aspiration to manifest our infinite potential result in a bloated ego and a sense of aggrandizement? We will address this question in the next section.

## True Growth Makes Us Humble

In so many walks of life, we see insatiable pride driving people to strive for more and more fame and power. This is nothing but an ego trip. Is the desire for spiritual growth different from it? Or is it just another expression of our ego?

The difference is huge. In fact, inner growth diminishes arrogance and replaces it with humility. Take the case of knowledge. It is said: *vidyā dadāti vinayaṁ* 'True knowledge brings humility.' The great scientist, Sir Isaac Newton, said, 'I was like a boy playing on the seashore … finding a smoother pebble or a prettier shell … whilst the great ocean of truth lay all undiscovered before me.'

Christian saint, Saint Augustine, called it 'learned ignorance'. He explained that those who are ignorant are also unaware of the magnitude of their ignorance, and as a result, they believe they know everything. True learning brings us in touch with our ignorance, and this makes us humble.

Saint Bhartrihari, disciple of the great yogi, Gorakhnath, expressed similar thoughts:

*yadā kiñcijjño 'haṁ gaja iva madāndhaḥ samabhavam*
*tadā sarvajño 'smītyabhavadavaliptaṁ mama manaḥ*
*yadā kiñchitkiñchid budhajanasakāśhādavagataṁ*
*tadā mūrkho 'smīti jvara iva mado me vyapagataḥ*

(*Nīti Shatak*, verse 8)

'When I knew little, then with pride bloated like an elephant, I thought I was all-knowing. But when I associated with saintly people and got a bit of wisdom, my conceit was shattered, and I understood that I am such a fool.'

In Plato's account of Socrates, we find a similar statement: 'I neither know nor think that I know.' (*Apology* 21D)

It is said of Socrates that he was asked what he knew. He replied that when he was young, he felt he knew everything, but now in his old age, he realized he knew only one thing, that he knew nothing.

Similarly, true inner growth puts us in touch with the insignificance of the individual soul before the magnificence of God's glory, and that makes us humble. We realize that even though our soul has infinite potential, before the glory of God, it will remain infinitesimal even at the zenith of its spiritual evolution.

Let me give you a little peek into the magnitude of God's creation. Modern science informs us that our earth is only one of the eight planets revolving around the Sun. Like it, there are 100 billion suns in our galaxy, the Milky Way. But this is not the only galaxy either. Like the Milky Way, there are a 100 billion galaxies in the universe. This means, there are $10^{22}$ suns in the entire universe.

But the matter does not even end there. Recent discoveries in astronomy point to the multiverse theory of many universes. This modern theory is only confirming what the Vedic scriptures stated 5,000 years ago. Let me share a story regarding this from the *Chaitanya Charitāmṛit.*

*In the age of Dwāpar, when Lord Krishna was residing in Dwarika, the secondary creator, Brahma, came to meet Him. Brahmaji said to the gatekeeper, 'Please inform the King of Dwarika that Brahma wishes to have His darshan.'*

*The guard conveyed the message to Shree Krishna, who replied, 'Ask him which Brahma is he.'*

*The doorkeeper returned to Brahmaji and said, 'Lord Krishna wishes to know which Brahma are you?'*

*Brahmaji was astonished on hearing the question because, in his understanding, he was the only Brahma. Nevertheless, he said to the sentinel, 'Tell Him that I am the creator of the universe, the four-headed Brahma.'*

*On receiving this answer, Lord Krishna asked for Brahmaji to be brought in. Brahmaji came before the Lord and offered his respectful obeisance. But his very first question was, 'O Most Respected One, what was the import of Your question, "Which Brahma?" Are there any other Brahmas apart from myself?'*

*Lord Krishna smiled. By His Yogamaya power He called all the Brahmas over to Dwarika. Now our four-headed Brahma got to see innumerable Brahmas arriving and offering their respects to Dwarikadhish.*

*The four-headed Brahma saw that there was one Brahma arriving who had 1,000 heads. He thought to himself, 'How large would his universe be?'*

*But there was also a Brahma coming who had one lakh (100,000) heads. How big would his universe be?*

*And then there were Brahmas arriving with one crore (ten million) heads. What would be the expanse of their creation?*

*Finally, there were Brahmas arriving with one arab (one billion) heads. How huge would be their dominion?!*

*Seeing this spectacle, Chaturmukhī (four-headed) Brahma fell at the feet of the Lord and begged to be forgiven. Lord Krishna then explained to him, 'Brahmaji, like your universe, there are innumerable such universes in My creation. Each has one Brahma in it. Yours is the smallest of them.'*

The story highlights the vastness of God's creation. However, all these universes referred to are within the material creation.

The Bhagavad Gita informs us that the material realm is only one-fourth of Creation. Three-fourths is the divine realm, which includes *Devi Lok, Golok, Saket Lok, Shiv Lok,* and *Vaikunth*. Now we can well imagine how tiny our earth planet is in creation!

Therefore, there is no need to worry that spiritual growth will make us proud. Rather, it will put us in touch with our minuteness in the grand scheme of things. That is why saints from all religious traditions around the world have expressed the deepest sentiments of humility in their writings.

Jagadguru Kripaluji Maharaj wrote: '*bhayo ko, mo sama patita baṛo*' (Could there be a more fallen soul than me?)

Saint Tulsidas wrote: '*mo sama kauna kuṭila khala kāmī*' (Who would be more wicked, deceitful, and desirous than me?)

Saint Soordas wrote: '*hari hauṅ saba patitana kau nāyaka*' (O Krishna, amongst all fallen souls, I am the worst.)

These sentiments expressed by saints are not hyperboles of speech. These are their genuine emotions that arise because they feel they still lack in comparison to the infinite graces they have received from God. In this way, inner growth and humility progress together.

## Our Golden Chance in Life

According to the Vedas, there are 8.4 million species of life corresponding to the different levels of consciousness. Since innumerable past lifetimes, our soul has been transmigrating from one body to the next. After many such lives, we have received the human form, as stated in the Ramayan:

*kabahuñka kari karuṇā nara dehī,*
*deta īsa binu hetu sanehī*

'Once in a while, causelessly merciful Lord bestows on the soul the human form. In it, we get the free will to decide our evolutionary growth.'

The other life forms—plants, birds, animals, fish, etc.—possess practically zero free will. Their diet, behaviours, inclinations, and mating patterns are all determined by the programming of their genetic code. We can observe the behaviour of so many migratory birds in India. When summer approaches they know they fly north—to Siberia, a distant land they have never seen. They will not fly south or east or west; they have no choice in this matter. The choice was predetermined by the programming of their DNA.

However, we humans have been given the dignity of choice. We can decide what to do, what to think, what to eat, and what to wear. Yet the paradox is that, except for humans, all life forms strive to their maximum potential.

How big do trees grow? As big as they can—as much as the nourishment in the ground, air, and water around will permit them to grow.

It is only us humans who stop growing. Why? Because we have the freedom of choice. We can choose to ignore opportunities; we can choose to pursue diversions; we can even choose to go downwards in our evolution. That is why the Vedas caution us to choose carefully!

*iha chedavedīdatha satyamasti na chedihā vedīnmahatī vinaṣhṭiḥ* (*Kenopaniṣhad* 2.5)

'O Humans! In this life form achieve the supreme goal. Or else you will continue transmigrating in the cycle of life and death.'

The Law of Infinite Potential, discussed in this first chapter, helped us decide the goal of our life. To move in that direction, we will now need knowledge of the second divine law, which is discussed in the next chapter.

## Key Takeaways

- The grand plan of Creation is the evolution of the soul towards supreme perfection.
- The immanence of God's glory is infinite. As His little fragments, we too possess infinite potential for growth.
- Growth does not happen automatically. It ensues when we commit ourselves to excellence in all our endeavours.
- Those with the fixed mindset believe their skills are determined by destiny or circumstance and cannot be developed any further.
- Those with the growth mindset realize that with proper effort, there is unlimited scope for progress.
- Under maya, our intellect suffers from three fallacies of understanding. These make us establish worthless goals, by which we short-change ourselves and do not make true progress.
- Divine knowledge helps us dispel these misconceptions, and then we develop faith in the infinite potential of our soul.
- When we grow from within, we realize the tininess of our soul before the splendour of God. Hence, true growth makes us humble.

# 2

# The Law of Incremental Growth

We all want success, accomplishment, and triumph, but what is the path to them? Is success an event that happens to us one fine day? Is accomplishment a neatly packed object that arrives at our doorstep like our mail? Does triumph descend out of the blue from the sky like lightning from the clouds?

The answer to all these questions is in the negative. These are all fanciful thoughts, far removed from the reality of life. Success is not an occurrence which happens at one point in time; it is a journey that is undertaken, one fruitful step at a time.

## Give Up the Lottery Winning Mentality

We have all heard stories of instant success. We are told of the railway ticket conductor who became an all-time cricket great; the martial arts instructor who became a Bollywood superstar; the young man who dropped out of Harvard to establish a corporate empire. And we have seen dozens of advertisements of people who went on crash diets and developed attractive figures in thirty days – flat.

Such popular stories convince us that fame or success will knock on our door sometime in future, so we might as well wait for that lucky day to come by. But this is like pinning our hopes on becoming rich by winning the Dubai lottery. The chances of it happening are of the order of 0.0000001. If you round that up to one decimal place, it is a big 'zero'. Would you be willing to gamble your life on such a chance?

**Human life is too precious to risk on the draw of a lottery. The reliable path to victory is forged by dedicated hard work, day after day, week after week, month after month, year after year.**

In fact, a background check of the so-called overnight successes, whose stories are so popular in society, often reveals that they too did not suddenly become lucky. Rather, they attracted luck by their immense hard work. As an example, let us look at the story of Bill Gates. It has been highlighted by Malcolm Gladwell in his book, *The Outliers.*

*William Henry Gates III, or Bill Gates, as he is known, grew up in a well-to-do suburb of Seattle. His parents realized that studies at his school were not engaging enough, so when he was in seventh grade, they shifted him to Lakeside, a private school for the wealthy. Next year, the school purchased a computer terminal hooked in real-time to a General Electric computer in downtown Seattle.*

*Bill Gates took great interest in the programming language, BASIC, and began spending twenty to thirty hours every week at the school computer centre. It literally took up all his free time after-school and during weekends. He even created a computer game called 'tic-tac-toe'.*

*But the school ran out of purchased computer time from the mainframe, which was awfully expensive in those days, and Gates and friends were left without access to computers. Fortunately, Computer Center Corporation (CCC) gave them free computer time in exchange for fixing bugs. The arrangement continued for nine months, until CCC went out of business, and Gates was again without access to computers.*

*The next chance came when Gates and friends were contacted by Information Systems Incorporated (ISI), which allowed them to work on their computer in exchange for automating the company payroll. The arrangement provided them 2,000 hours of online programming time during the next few months.*

*The plan only ended when they stole company passwords and crashed the entire system. As a result, ISI threw them out. Next, they began frequenting the computer centre of the University of Washington, which allowed free access from 3 a.m. to 6 a.m. every morning.*

*Next year, Lakeside School was contacted by TRW, a technology company that had recently purchased a computer for their power station. Gates and friends were allowed by the school to camp at the TRW site, and they spent the entire spring writing code.*

*On graduating from school, Bill Gates entered Harvard. One day he read in the magazine* Popular Electronics *that Micro Instrumentation and Telemetry Systems (MITS) needed a BASIC interpreter programme for their platform. That was when he dropped out of college to work on the software. He established Microsoft and began leasing the software to MITS and others.*

After reading Bill Gates' story above, it would be naïve to say that he woke up one fine day and discovered he was blessed with computer expertise. Rather, he reached that level of mastery by dedicating himself to writing programmes—every hour of the day he could spare in middle and high school—consistently over a period of five years.

Someone may say, 'Why have you given Bill Gates' example? Are you not aware of the unethical practices he adopted to succeed in business?' Well, the purpose of including his story is not to justify or eulogize everything he did, but to illustrate the simple truth that proficiency in any field is the consequence of consistent dedication and hard work. There is a popular Sanskrit saying:

*kṣhaṇasaḥ kṣhaṇaso vidyā kaṇasaḥ kaṇaso dhanam*

This verse states that you do not become a billionaire suddenly; you do so by earning little bits of money and continuing to do it over time. Likewise, you cannot become a scholar in one go; you do so by using individual moments, again and again, to gather knowledge. This is the principle of incremental growth.

When we see people super-proficient in their field, we wonder how they got there. The answer is invariably the same—by repeatedly taking small steps in the proper direction. So, the rule of life is (and I am modifying the Chinese philosopher Lao Tzu's words here):

- A magnificent architectural monument does not manifest suddenly; it is built by gradually assembling its individual blocks.
- A long journey is not completed in a single leap but by traversing its smaller individual segments.

Similarly, **one does not transform from a sinner to a saint overnight, but by making the proper choices, again and again, repeatedly over time.**

Let us see what kind of choices we have.

## The Choices We Make

What lies between the letters 'B' and 'D'? The letter 'C' of course. But this simple sequence of three letters can also be used to depict a profound truth of life. Between 'Birth' and 'Death' are the 'Choices' we make.

The details of our birth were not determined by us. We did not choose our country of birth; nor did we have a say in deciding our mother tongue or parents. Nobody asked us which colour of skin, eyes, and hair we would prefer. Birth was a pre-decided affair. We will not select the variables of our death either—the mode, time, or date.

Between these two determinates of birth and death, the field of life unfolds and presents us with an array of choices. We select our thoughts, priorities, emotions, and behaviours. **Regardless of how good or bad we may presently be, we can always choose to make our future better. Regrettably, we also have the option of choosing to make our future worse.**

Every choice veers our life up or down one teeny-weeny bit. By itself, the individual moments do not seem to count for much. But as they accumulate with time, the difference becomes significant.

*Compare the life trajectory of two classmates. For now, let us call them Sat and Ram. It is the year 1980, and both study in a school that few outside Telangana have heard of—Hyderabad Public School.*

*Sat is an average performer at academics. He is not naturally brilliant, but he makes up for it by consistently choosing hard work over pleasure. On graduating from school, he fails to crack the Joint Entrance Exam (JEE) of the prestigious IITs. But he does manage to get admission to an average engineering school—Manipal Institute of Technology.*

*Now let us look at his classmate, Ram. He is genetically highly intelligent but believes in having fun. He loves reading trashy novels and frequenting movie halls with likeminded friends. He can be found at 10 p.m. every night at the tea stall in his neighbourhood. Yet, by virtue of his inborn brilliance, he sails through the JEE and joins the prestigious IIT Madras.*

*Thirty years later, guess who is more successful? Surprisingly, it is Sat. He is the head of a corporation that employs 130,000 people worldwide. The work he does enriches the quality of life of 1.5 billion people around the globe. On the other hand, Ram, his former classmate, has just lost yet another sales job and is searching for a new one.*

*How did the career and life trajectories of Sat and Ram diverge so extraordinarily in three decades? Well, let me tell you their real names. Sat is actually Satya Nadella, the CEO of Microsoft Corporation. Though he was a mediocre student in school, by virtue of his diligent nature, he kept plodding upward. In college he was no longer considered mediocre. Rather, he was now considered proficient and was selected for the Master's in Computer Science program at University of Wisconsin in Milwaukee. Later when he got a job at Microsoft Corporation, he chose to do an MBA alongside. He would fly out of Silicon Valley on Friday nights to attend classes at the University of Chicago during weekends. His outstanding mindset and growing skillset got him noticed at Microsoft. He utilized every opportunity he received to learn and to deliver results. Finally, when Steve Ballmer resigned, the Microsoft Board did not hesitate to announce that Satya Nadella would be the next CEO of the company.*

*Now let us come to Sat's classmate, Ram. He is actually Ramu Mithyavardhanulu. Ramu who? That is precisely my point. You have never heard of him because he never did anything of significance despite graduating from one of the best engineering colleges in India.*

What was the secret of Satya Nadella's amazing success story? It could not have been innate intelligence, else Ramu Mithyavardhanulu would have surpassed him any day. It was his consistency in choosing growth over pleasure, and meaningful work over frivolous enjoyment. When this formula was repeated hundreds of moments daily, for 365 days every year, over a period of thirty years, it resulted in an ordinary student becoming the world-renowned Satya Nadella whom we all are familiar with today. Ramu Mithyavardhanulu had the same, or possibly even greater, potential in him. But he squandered it away, one poor choice at a time.

This comparison of the trajectory of life of two schoolmates, over a period of three decades, illustrates the second divine law:

---

## The Law of Incremental Growth

*Personal excellence and life mastery can only be achieved by consistent small steps of incremental improvement.*

---

This principle applies to all fields of human activity. People come and ask me, 'Swamiji, I wish to attach my mind to God, but it continually drifts away. Why does this happen?' I explain to them that having the mind completely absorbed in God is siddhi, or the state of perfection. If the scriptures expected us to become a siddha on the first day of the journey itself, then why would they instruct us to do sadhana? We must be willing to begin the path from the first rung of the ladder.

Accomplishment in any field is not a gift from Creation; it must be earned through dedicated effort. Hence, the *Yoga Sutras* state:

*tīvrasaṁvegānām āsannaḥ* (*Samādhi Pāda* 1.14)

'Success in sadhana comes quickly to those who are intensely vigorous and energetic in practice.'

Nowadays, there is no dearth of advertisements promising you an annual income of two crore rupees if you simply spend two hours daily on the internet; weight loss of twenty kilos by wearing a special belt; and perfection in meditation if you take initiation in a particular mantra. Surprisingly, people are willing to get duped into believing these alluring marketing lines.

*Many years ago, an advertisement appeared in a newspaper in Kolkata, 'Learn 3-Minute Dhyānam'. It promised guaranteed success in meditation within three minutes. This episode happened in the 1960s, when religious sentiments ran deeper amongst the Indian populace.*

*The advertisement attracted a huge crowd. At the appointed hour, a gathering of 1,000 people had collected in the street outside the venue. The consequence was that the police had to be called to bring the situation under control. Unfortunately, apprehending a stampede, the police resorted to lathi charge. The people who had come for 3-Minute Dhyānam ended up with bruised limbs from the lathi blows.*

The problem is that **our human nature wants quick fixes—excellence without toil and perfection without practice. But life mastery and enlightenment are not cheap bargains. They are achieved through sacrifice, dedication, and perseverance.**

Jagadguru Shree Kripaluji Maharaj used to say that if you tried meditation, and on the first day you succeeded only one minute in ten, do not be discouraged. Keep up your practice. The next week, you will find you are able to meditate two minutes in ten. The following week it will be three minutes in ten. And once you cross the fifty per cent mark, further progress will be a breeze. This is the Law of Incremental Growth.

The good news is that the level of difficulty does not remain the same throughout the journey. In fact, every incremental step becomes easier than the previous one. This happens because of a phenomenon we will discuss next.

## Behavioural Momentum

Social scientists have discovered a concept called behavioural momentum. We are familiar with the momentum of solid objects. You may have had the experience of pushing someone's car. When the engine does not turn on with the ignition switch, passengers get out of the car and begin pushing it. Initially, your every muscle is exerted to overcome the vehicle's static inertia. But slowly, the movement begins and then keeps picking speed. When the driver sees the car has gathered enough momentum, she releases the clutch, to engage the engine with a jerk and kick start it.

This is an illustration of the momentum of physical objects. Interestingly, the same phenomenon applies to human behaviour as well. **As you strive to improve yourself, the velocity of your self-transformation keeps speeding up. The reason is that any learned behaviour becomes easier with every repetition, until it finally becomes a habit.**

For example, if you wish to wake up and meditate at 4 a.m., it may be an immense struggle on your first day, but as the weeks go by, the practice grows on you and becomes natural. As you keep practising, the impetus works in your favour. This is the behavioural momentum.

This term, Big Momentum, or 'the Big Mo', was initially used in the 1960s in connection with sporting events in the US. It was discovered that when teams won a few successive matches, they would continue the winning streak, as if impetus from their previous wins was helping them.

Presently, behavioural momentum is better understood due to greater insight into the functioning of the brain. The science of neurology explains that whenever we do any mental or physical work, our brain fires up neurons in the sensory motor region, neocortex, and prefrontal cortex. But, interestingly, the human brain is such a self-programming mechanism that when it realizes a task is being done repeatedly, it creates neural programmes to ease its work.

That is how you develop proficiency in so many commonplace tasks, such as typing. It seems as if you do not need to think where the key for each letter is. Our fingers literally fly on the keyboard at blurring speeds. Can you really hit the correct keys without thinking? Of course not! No work is possible without thinking. Then how did you acquire this proficiency? As you began practising typing, your brain noted the task being repeated. Then, to make its task easier, it stored programmes in the basal ganglia, thereby making the task easier and easier with time.

What was the secret of this acquired proficiency in typing? If a poor villager, with no prior exposure to keyboards, were to see you pressing the keys at such a speed, she would wonder how you manage it. Your fingers are moving faster than she can even imagine. The villager would likely conclude that you possess some miraculous yogic siddhi. But you know that it is a very commonplace skill acquired with just one year of practice. This is the habit-forming nature of the brain.

*An experiment was performed on mice by the Brain and Cognitive Sciences Department of the Massachusetts Institute of Technology (MIT) in the 1990s. The mice were left in a maze with equipment attached to their head to measure their brain activity. The maze had cheese at the other end, which the mice could smell but not see. While they sniffed their way to the cheese, their headgear measured the level of their brain activity.*

*It was observed that when the experiment was repeated daily, with the cheese at the same spot, the mice started getting to it faster and faster. Their headgear confirmed that their brainwork for the task was getting progressively reduced. The brain was creating programmes—networks and neural pathways—to automate the work for itself.*

The human brain has a similar habit-forming nature. Maharshi Patanjali states in his famed *Yoga Sutras*:

*sa tu dīrgha-kāla nairantarya-satkārāsevito dṛiḍhabhūmiḥ*
(*Samādhi Pāda* 1.14)

'When practice is continued for long duration with dedication and without interruption, it becomes firmly grounded in the mind as a habit.'

Slowly, the choices that we keep repeating, grow onto us and become a part of us. This is why it is said: 'First we make choices and then the choices make us.' Now, **if our choices are harmful, the momentum will build up in the wrong direction and work to our detriment. But if we keep repeating good choices, the impetus will develop in the beneficial direction and will work to our advantage.**

This explains why the most difficult part of any behavioural modification is the initial phase. It is when our brain is breaking the neural pathways of old habits and establishing circuitry for new ones. Once the behavioural momentum builds up, we reach the auto mode and enjoy the ride, because progress in life has almost reached the automatic level.

It is like sending a rocket into space. The maximum thrust is required in the initial few minutes when the rocket is breaking through the gravitational pull of the earth. After it gathers enough velocity, the fuel consumption reduces to a minimal amount. Similarly, once behavioural momentum develops, the process of life enhancement picks up ever-increasing pace.

In this manner, behavioural change goes through three stages:

1. ***Conscious Incompetence.*** In this stage, we struggle to learn a new skill, acquire a beneficial mindset, or develop a good habit. Or alternatively, we grapple to break a harmful habit long solidified within us. But despite consciously focusing and applying our intellect to the task, we are incompetent at it.

2. ***Conscious Competence.*** In the second stage, we have developed a moderate level of proficiency. We can now fulfil the task competently but only by focusing our complete attention on it.
3. ***Unconscious Competence.*** In this final stage, we discover we can perform the task adeptly even without paying full attention. The behavioural impetus is now with us.

Unfortunately, the same principle of momentum can work in the negative direction as well.

## Negative Momentum Can Ruin Your Life

*If you ever happen to meet compulsive drug addicts, you will be shocked to discover that many of them were at one time talented people from various walks of life. Ask them how they fell into such a state of wretchedness and they will tell you that it all started off very innocuously. When they were students, their friends offered them a joint of cannabis. They smoked it casually, never imagining in their wildest dreams what they were getting into.*

*Soon, they were regularly smoking those 'joints', always with the belief that they could give them up whenever they wished. But the addiction slowly began taking grip, and they switched from cannabis to heroin.*

*Gradually, they found even smoking heroin did not suffice because the body and mind were demanding more. So, they converted to injecting the heroin into their veins and muscles, and that gave them the experience of a 'rush' of euphoria. But there was no end in sight because the body's need for the chemical kept growing.*

*Now, it was becoming expensive to procure the growing requirement of drug. The pocket money received from parents would run out quickly. Thus, they started stealing goods from home and selling them for their next 'fix'. Parents would wonder why items were suddenly missing. Then, the day came when even stealing from home did not suffice in meeting the ever-increasing need for fixes.*

*In the next step, boys took to peddling the drug, while girls took to selling their body for money. As parents and relatives came to know, there was social shame and psychological pain. Finally, at this late stage, realization dawned about the mess they had gotten into. They tried to get off the addiction, but now the behavioural momentum was against them. Even after multiple visits to the rehabilitation centre, it was a struggle to break the grip of the chemical addiction, which had all started innocently with a single joint.*

This is an extreme example of negative momentum. But the same mechanism works every time we human beings fall into an addiction. The Bhagavad Gita states:

*dhyāyato viṣhayān puṁsaḥ saṅgas teṣhūpajāyate*
*saṅgāt sañjāyate kāmaḥ kāmāt krodho 'bhijāyate* (2.62)

'While contemplating on the objects of the senses, one develops attachment to them. Attachment leads to desire, and from desire arises anger.'

The hardcore alcoholic never imagined that his social drinking would one day grab him so firmly that over-drinking would cause him cirrhosis of liver. The casual internet surfer did not anticipate that frequent visits to inappropriate sites would result in an addiction to pornography. The inveterate gambler could not foresee that, in the future, the itch to wager would trouble her every evening.

These are only a few samples; chemical and behavioural additions are of all kinds. We find middle schoolers addicted to video games and grownups addicted to 'binge eating' for solace. Many suffer from 'exercise addiction' and spend irrational amounts of time on it. We hear of consumers who believe in 'shop till you drop'. Yet others are victims of 'tattoo addiction'. And many more such trappings.

The signs of a behaviour reaching addictive levels are:

- Becoming dependent upon the behaviour to cope with emotions.
- Continuing the behaviour despite physical and/or mental harm.
- Having trouble cutting back despite wanting to stop.
- Neglecting work, school, or family to engage in the behaviour.
- Experiencing symptoms of withdrawal (like depression and irritability) when trying to stop.
- Minimizing or hiding the extent of the problem.

The pity is that all behavioural addictions were like little saplings at the outset, but they grew into huge trees with repeated indulgence. **Hence, the best way to get rid of an addiction is to never start it in the first place; or having started become aware and desist right away.** Else, the more you delay getting off it, the harder it will become.

We have discussed behavioural momentum and its impact upon us, for better or for worse. Let us now draw some obvious and important conclusions from this analysis.

**Question**: How can we lift our life to great heights?

**Answer**: By creating behavioural impetus in the proper direction. Once the momentum works in our favour, we will soon be flying at high altitudes. Believe it or not, it is as simple as that!

**Question**: How can we build good momentum in connection with who we are and what we do?

**Answer**: Again, the answer is so simple! By consistently making good choices, one good choice at a time. We learned this in the second divine law, the principle of incremental growth.

**Question**: What is the secret to making good choices?

**Answer**: Yes, that is the obvious next question. Let us now discuss the solution to it.

## Good Choices Require Sacrifice

Success in any field requires sacrificing immediate pleasure for long-term benefit. Remember some of the sacrifices we made in life?

- When we were in school and wanted good grades, we sacrificed extra hours of play to spend time studying our textbooks. We knew that getting good grades was painful. We had to choose between the pain of intense study now or the pain of remaining mediocre in life.
- When we were young and wanted to build muscles, we tolerated discomfort to do a few extra push-ups. We knew that building the body was painful. We had to choose between the pain of exerting the body now or the embarrassment of a poor physique later.
- When we wanted the promotion at office, we stayed up late at night to prepare the powerpoint for our boss. We knew

that getting ahead in our career was painful. But we had to choose between the pain of the hard work now or the pain of stagnating in our career in the future.

- When we wanted to get our weight under control, we stayed off the ras malais, pastries, and gulab jamuns. Resisting the temptation was painful, but we knew that good health would require sacrifice. The choice we had was between bearing the pain of restraining the senses now or living with the pain of ill health later.
- When our good friend was upset and not willing to talk to us, we took the humble position and apologized. It was painful to suppress our ego, but we knew that maintaining the friendship would require sacrifice. Our choice was whether to bear the pain of crushing our pride or the pain of losing a friend.

Our lifetime experience tells that progress and lasting joy do not come easy. We must be willing to undergo austerity and discomfort. **The choice we have is whether to bear the good kind of pain that leads to progress, prosperity, knowledge, and enlightenment; or to choose the wrong kind of pain that is initially pleasurable, but later results in stagnation, ill health, ignorance, and discontentment.**

It was Mark Twain who observed: 'The only way to keep your health is to eat what you don't want, drink what you don't like, and do what you'd rather not.' Maybe Twain was being cynical, but what he said holds a lot of weight. Good health requires sacrificing gratification and the willingness to do unpleasant things.

Consider the example of the amla (Indian gooseberry). It is a unique superfood endowed with immense power to boost our immunity. A single amla has the vitamin C of ten oranges and is also rich in antioxidants. But the catch is that it is bitter to taste. It often happens that a mother offers amla to her child, but the child refuses to eat since it is so unpleasant. The mother then explains: *āmle kā khāyā aur baroṅ kā kahā, bād meṅ patā chaltā hai* 'My child, you will realize the value of eating amla and the benefit of elders' advice later.'

That is why, to choose well, willpower is such an imperative virtue in life, for it enables us to lead a disciplined life, in tune with our highest values. Let us look at it next.

## The Importance of Willpower

Invariably, situations present us with two kinds of choices: the 'pleasurable' and the 'beneficial'. Whatever we choose, there are consequences to reap or suffer, as the case may be:

1. Choosing the 'pleasurable' is initially gratifying but later results in unfulfillment and the guilt of unmanifest potential.
2. Choosing the 'beneficial' is initially unpleasant but later bestows growth and the inner contentment that comes from knowing we did our best.

The choice between these is ours. Good choices are what distinguish the 'successful' from the 'failures'. The successful choose hard work, persistence, and austerity. The failures find these unpleasant and avoid them. The successful also find them unpleasant but choose them nevertheless. The point to note is that **effective people do not give importance to their likes and dislikes; instead, they prioritize their sense of purpose and choose accordingly**. If the failures could also learn to make beneficial choices, even though unpleasant, they would also start becoming successful.

Hence, the crowning virtues in life are self-discipline and willpower. So many problems that people face can be correlated to their lack of self-control. Obesity, alcoholism, irrational spending, drug addiction, lack of exercise, fits of anger, malingering in school, and insincerity at work are just a few of them.

The external barriers to success are small; the biggest barriers are our own laziness, indiscipline, and intemperance. Author and educator James Thom expressed this so well, 'Probably the most honest self-made man ever was the one we heard say: "I got to the top the hard way—fighting my own laziness and ignorance every step of the way."'

Thus, to learn to become more self-disciplined is one of the most rewarding endeavours in life. This faculty of willpower is very much like a muscle, which contracts when unused and expands when exercised. **We weaken our willpower muscle every time we know the correct course of action but fail to choose it because of laziness or temptation.** Similarly, every time we choose what is right knowing fully well that it is difficult and unpleasant, we strengthen our willpower muscle.

Building willpower is thus like weaving a cable of steel—you keep adding individual strands of wire to it. Finally, the cable grows so strong that, in shipping dockyards, it can even lift thousands of tons of weight into the air. Similarly, willpower too can be enhanced until it becomes like a shield protecting us from the allurements and distractions all around.

In my previous book, *7 Mindsets for Success, Happiness, and Fulfilment* (2019), I detailed the science of willpower and how to develop it through various exercises. These help us grow the subtle muscle of self-control in the prefrontal cortex region of our brain.

Apart from exercises in the book, there are other simple exercises that you can set up for yourself. If you are habituated to drinking coffee, test your self-restraint by staying off it for a month, simply to grow your willpower muscle. On the third day, your mind and senses will be screaming, 'This is torture! It is unfair upon us.' But do not give in. Soon, you will find it becoming easier. As a result, you will become a more self-controlled person.

If you are addicted to entertaining your intellect with world news and current affairs, then your willpower exercise can possibly be to avoid all news media for a month. Do not worry about what will happen to the planet—it will continue to rotate—but you will grow in self-discipline.

**The nature of the mind and senses is such that if you give them an inch, they want a mile. But if you practice taming them with firm determination, they soon subside, and you become a better person.**

However, a word of caution is necessary. No matter how much we enhance it, willpower is still a limited faculty, and it is insufficient armoury for facing the challenges of maya all around us. In contrast, the material energy, maya, being God's energy, is infinitely powerful. Its ability to distract, tempt, and lure is enormous. Thus, nobody can ever claim that 'maya can never tempt me.' Even great yogis, rishis, and ascetics find themselves falling short in self-restraint before the lures of the world.

If we wish to reach our supreme goal, we will have to look for a force even greater than willpower. What is that? It is the 'why-power', which according to the Vedas, is far superior. Unleashing it will result in multiplying our self-control manifold. We discuss it in the next chapter.

## Key Takeaways

- The lottery-winning mentality that success will happen to us one day must be given up.
- Personal excellence and life mastery can only be achieved by consistent small steps of incremental improvement.
- At every moment, life presents us with choices. Every choice veers our life up or down one teeny-weeny bit. As the results of our choices accumulate, the difference becomes significant.
- The most difficult part of any behavioural modification is the initial phase. Later, with the help of behavioural momentum, the speed of our self-transformation increases.
- Unfortunately, the same principle of momentum can work in the negative direction as well and ruin our life.
- We must learn to choose the good kind of pain that leads to progress and wellbeing; not the wrong kind of pain that results in stagnation and ill health.
- To learn to become more self-disciplined is one of the most rewarding endeavours in life.
- The faculty of willpower is very much like a muscle, which contracts when unused and expands when exercised.
- No matter how much we enhance it, willpower is still a limited faculty and is insufficient for facing the challenges around us.

# 3

# The Law of Beliefs

FROM TIME to time, we all become painfully aware of the insufficiency of our willpower. With utmost self-control, we stick to a health-enhancing diet for two weeks, but then lose control one day and indulge in binge eating. We resolve not to waste time on social media, and even adhere to it for ten days. But on the eleventh day, we realize our self-control has busted; then three hours go by surfing purposelessly on the internet. We practice holding our tongue in control and speaking sweetly to all for a fortnight. But a week later, someone's irritable behaviour goes beyond our tolerance, and we lash out in rage.

On the one hand, the challenges around us are enormous. On the other hand, our ability for self-restraint is limited. Is there any way of going beyond the constraining threshold of our 'willpower'?

There is, and the solution is to unleash the potential of 'why-power'.

# Going Beyond Willpower

What is 'why-power'? Let me share a personal experience of it.

*When I was in engineering college, I did not relish the academic syllabus. That is probably a statement not uncommon amongst students around the world, but I had an extra reason for it. In school I had loved humanities and language subjects, but unfortunately, I did well in science. Accordingly, well-wishers innocently pushed me into an engineering college. I compounded the blunder by selecting mechanical engineering as my branch of specialization, where I had to encounter lathe machines, sheet metal workshops, iron foundries, and combustion engines.*

*As a result, while my mind was looking for tranquillity, serenity, and harmony, I ended up negotiating an environment of cranky machines, copper filings, and shrieking steam. Naturally, willpower was in short supply, and on scores of occasions I skipped labs and lectures. I preferred sitting in the campus library to read books on poetry instead of breaking my head over equations in thermodynamics postulating the axial temperature gradient in gas turbine compressors. Estimably, about half the students in class were equally insincere, each for their own individual reasons.*

*However, semester after semester, and year after year, an interesting pattern revealed itself. On the night before the exams, all the students in the hostel, including myself, could be found in their rooms, wholly engrossed in academics, studying away through the night. Where did the self-discipline suddenly come from? These students did not possess such mind control on other days of the year.*

*Well, the source of the sudden ability for self-abnegation was not 'willpower' but 'why-power'. The students reasoned, 'If I succumb to the pleasure of sleeping early tonight, I will flunk my exam tomorrow. This cannot be allowed to happen; I must stay awake and study, no matter how much my mind and senses scream that it is unpleasant.'*

This was an example of 'why-power', which refers to the impetus that arises when we are deeply motivated. **If we become convinced of an imperative reason for doing something, we suddenly find hidden reserves of energy to perform herculean tasks.**

*Suppose a building in your neighbourhood catches fire, and you are standing by, watching. The burning house's proprietor requests you to go in and help retrieve his valuables lying inside. You will emphatically refuse to take the risk, and even doubt whether he is crazy to expect you to do that.*

*But what if it was your own home that was burning, with your two-year-old daughter sleeping inside? Now that would change the scenario completely. Despite the intimidating flames, you would still find the courage to go into the inferno and save your little darling.*

How did you suddenly develop heroic qualities surpassing even those of fire fighters? It was the presence of a strong inspiration that ignited the best in you. The same power of motivation is what enables mothers to lift cars when they discover their baby under the car tyre.

These are all examples of 'why-power', which can make very ordinary people perform superhuman feats. Let us try to understand the basis of this power to see how we can tap into it.

## The Source of Why-power

We are divine souls, and the body is our external machinery. Our internal machinery, primarily, is the mind and intellect. People understand the importance of the mind and struggle to control it. But they do not realize that the intellect is even more critical to their well-being.

In the Bhagavad Gita, Lord Krishna instructs Arjun to manage both the mind and intellect:

*mayy eva mana ādhatsva mayi buddhiṁ niveśhaya*
*nivasiṣhyasi mayy eva ata ūrdhvaṁ na sanśhayaḥ* (12.8)

'Fix your mind on Me and surrender your intellect to Me. There upon, you will always live in Me. Of this, there is no doubt.'

As we can see above, the Bhagavad Gita instructs us to work upon both aspects of our inner machinery—the mind and intellect. **When we practice controlling our mind, that is the exercise of our *willpower*.** And **when we develop suitable beliefs in our intellect, that provides us with *why-power*.**

What is the reason that 'why-power' is stronger than 'willpower'? The *Yajur Veda* provides the answer:

*indriyebhyaḥ parā hyarthā arthebhyaśhca paraṁ manaḥ*
*manasastu parā buddhir buddherātmā mahān paraḥ*
(*Kaṭhopaniṣhad* 1.3.10)

'Beyond the physical senses are the objects of the senses; subtler than objects of the senses is the mind. Superior to the mind is the intellect, and beyond the intellect is the soul.'

This Upanishadic verse explains that the intellect is a faculty superior to the mind. Therefore, the beliefs we hold in our intellect can control the functioning of our mind. Let me give you another example of the power of the intellect relative to the mind.

*Suppose someone has a weakness for sweetmeats. But the doctor has warned him that his sugar count is in the prediabetic region, and he had better be careful. Consequently, he struggles to control his temptation. His mind and tongue yearn for the pleasure of sugar, which he finds hard to resist.*

*However, when that same person is about to indulge in his favourite jalebi, someone exclaims, 'There is poison in the jalebi. You will die if you eat it.'*

*Now the situation has changed drastically. The intellect immediately comes into action. It instructs the mind and the senses, 'The jalebi is extremely dangerous. It will result in death, so hold yourselves in check.'*

*Once the intellect decides, the mind and senses must obey. Come what may, that person will not eat the jalebi that he believes is laced with deadly poison.*

This is the strength of the intellect. When it decides to exert itself, the mind is obliged to become subservient to it. This illustration proves that—**amongst all the internal machinery we possess—the intellect is supreme.** And since beliefs are convictions of the intellect, they are enormously powerful. They can authoritatively command the functioning of both our subconscious and conscious mind.

Therefore, it is imperative to understand the role of beliefs in determining the quality and direction of our life.

# The Power of Beliefs

*A group of tourists was stranded in the countryside. They were given old rations to eat. Being doubtful about their edibility, they decided to test the food before consuming it. They fed it to a dog, who seemed to enjoy it and suffered no side effects. This convinced them that the food was safe, and they devoured it hungrily.*

*The next day, they learned that the dog had died. Everyone was spooked by the news. Many began vomiting and complaining of fever and dysentery. A doctor was called to treat the victims for food poisoning.*

*The doctor asked what happened to the body of the dog. Enquiries were made. A neighbour said casually, 'Oh, it was thrown into the ditch because it was run over by a car'. On hearing that the dog had not been poisoned by the food, the sick became miraculously well.*

This is the power of beliefs. They can make us well, and they can make us sick. If our intellect is fully convinced that we should be feeling ill, our subconscious behaves as if it were already true and connives to make us sick. The subconscious does not doubt what our intellect resolutely thinks to be true. Therefore, **whatever we strongly believe becomes our virtual reality, irrespective of whether it is true or not. And the stronger the intensity of our belief, the greater its influence over our emotions**. The legendary industrialist and business magnate, Henry Ford, very rightly said: 'If you believe that you can do a thing, or if you believe you cannot, in either case, you are right'.

Without realizing it, we limit ourselves by our own beliefs. When a teacher is firmly convinced that she does not have the qualifications to become school principal, her own subconscious sabotages her chances for promotion and becomes her own worst enemy. External enemies can be identified and addressed. But in this case, the enemy is inconspicuously sitting within, in the form of her incorrect convictions. That is what makes them so much more dangerous.

On the other hand, when we fervently believe in the Law of Infinite Potential, our subconscious gets to work for our ascent in life. We all know the immensely inspiring example of a tea seller who rose to become the Prime Minister of India. What contributed to his amazing rise? If he had thought that selling tea was all that he was born for, he would not have even dreamed of doing anything more significant. However, he must have held a vision deep within him that his life was meant for more valuable things. His belief catapulted him upward, to the point where he got the opportunity to serve 1.3 billion people or 17.7 per cent of the world population.

Thus, we can see how beliefs are the biggest force within our personality that can work to our benefit or detriment. With that clarity, we now come to the third divine law:

---

## The Law of Beliefs

*The trajectory of our life is determined by the beliefs we hold in our intellect.*

---

If you believe that money is of paramount importance, you will naturally spend your life gathering every rupee you can. Instead, if you are convinced that social prestige matters most, then you will blow up your money for the sake of winning elections. And if you believe that love for God is the highest treasure, you will spend your time in devotional pursuits.

**We think we walk by sight, but factually, the course of our life gets determined by our beliefs.** Let me again share a personal example—the trajectory of my own life.

*As I travel around the world, one question is posed to me almost daily. 'Swamiji, you graduated from IIT and IIM. Then what happened to you that you took such an extreme step of renouncing the world and accepting sanyas?' People expect me to share some tragic episode that changed the course of my life.*

*But my answer comes to them as an anti-climax. I tell them, 'The only thing that happened was this: I believed the knowledge I am sharing with you.'*

*'Really, that is all?' they ask, surprised.*

*'Yes. I believed that I am not the body made of matter but the divine soul. I also believed that my soul is a fragmental part of God. And so, I decided that the purpose of my life should be to serve my Eternal Relative.'*

*People then respond, 'But we also believe that we are souls and tiny parts of God. Why does a similar spiritual yearning not ignite in us?'*

*'Well, it means you do not really believe it, for if you did, then you too would have experienced a similar spiritual calling to make God as the topmost priority in your life. Remember, there is a difference between knowing and believing. We know so many things, but the question is how deeply do we believe them?'*

So, as I was saying earlier, the direction of our life gets mapped by our convictions. Whether we believe we are the body or the soul, whether we believe in the Law of Karma and so on, our values will be determined by it. Thus, it becomes imperative that we choose our beliefs well.

## Bad Beliefs Can Ruin Our Life

Beliefs work like a double-edged sword. Good beliefs empower us for ever-increasing success, while bad beliefs impair us like nothing else. For example, if you have faith that merit gets rewarded in the workplace, you will be inspired to strive for professional mastery. If, instead, you are convinced that promotion in the office is all a matter of politics, naturally you will be unenthused to play your best game.

The disheartenment here is not a salary issue, or a harsh work environment, or anything else. It is merely a false belief that 'manipulation, not merit, determines promotion'. What a pity! The work situation is congenial for growth, but the enemy—incorrect conviction—is sitting inside. Therefore, **let us commit this aphorism to memory: Nothing can ruin us in life more than our own incorrect bad beliefs.**

Every so often, parents approach me, 'Swamiji, my teenage son has gone astray. He is gripped by the awful vice of narcotic addiction. What should I do?'

I reply, 'Check his friends circle. If his close acquaintances are derelicts, his beliefs have been adversely impacted. In association with drug addicts, he has become convinced that shunning responsibility and experiencing the euphoric "high" from drugs is the definition of a good life. That defective belief is destroying him.'

As they say in Hindi: *saṅga kā raṅga paṛatā hai* 'Our beliefs get coloured by the company we keep.' This is particularly relevant for teenagers, who are more impressionable, since their own convictions are yet tender. Thus, it is vitally important for youngsters to choose friends who value hard work, sincerity, and dedication.

*The threat of bad beliefs prevails even in adulthood because of the ignorance within us. People ask me, 'Swamiji, why is it that those who do good are the ones who suffer in life, while those who do bad are so happy?'*

*I caution them, 'Please do not think like this ever again. If this is your faith, then you too will want to be a bad person because you will be convinced it will bring you happiness.*

*'Factually, your evaluation is defective. You are looking at the externals and concluding so-and-so person is happy because she has a big home and car. If you could look within, you would say, "Ram ... Ram ... Ram ... I am much better off than her."'*

**So be more careful about the beliefs you hold in your head than the food you put in your mouth.** Albert Einstein explained that people can have two kinds of beliefs about the universe in which we live: 'The most important decision we make is whether we believe we live in a friendly or hostile universe.'

Some believe that Creation is malevolent. They are convinced there is no fairness and justice in the events that occur in life. They are firmly of the view that the world is an awful place to live in. Accordingly, they see misery, insufficiency, and harassment everywhere.

In contrast are those who look on the world as benevolent. They are convinced that life is a tremendous opportunity bestowed upon the soul. They have faith that the Universe possesses abundance and there is plenty for all who strive for it. They see the good in others. They are optimistic about situations and hopeful for the future. It goes without saying that the optimists are the ones who receive more blessings and move ahead. The pessimists blame their luck without realizing they enticed it to themselves.

We have discussed the importance of avoiding bad beliefs. But what is the process? How can we eradicate detrimental beliefs and develop productive ones in their place? Let us discuss this next.

## The Way to Good Beliefs

The tragedy is that we simply allow beliefs to happen to us. For example, we pick some opinions from our environment. As they say in the US, 'The children of Democrats are Democrats, and the children of Republicans are Republicans.' People's beliefs about politics are determined more by family environment than by deep analysis.

Other beliefs are developed only because we hear something repeatedly.

*Joseph Goebbels, minister of propaganda in Hitler's regime, knew the power of repeating falsehoods. He asserted: 'If you tell a lie and keep repeating it, people will eventually come to believe it.' The biggest tragedy of the twentieth century was caused by the Nazis' use of this theory to dupe the German nation into believe gross untruths and then leading them into the Second World War.*

This was an extreme case of misbeliefs by the power of repetition. But the danger of developing unhealthy beliefs is all around. In this cyber age, the situation is even more complex. Fake news, videos, and images get circulated among millions on social media platforms in fractions of seconds. As someone said: 'A lie can travel halfway round the world, while the truth is still putting on its shoes.' Before facts get a chance, the lie has already been accepted as the truth.

Such hearsay is a disastrous way of creating our faith system. The simple logic is that wrong knowledge leads to wrong beliefs and good knowledge leads to good beliefs. **To develop perfect beliefs, we must get perfect knowledge from a trustworthy source.** That is the first step. This is called *śhravaṇam*, or hearing. In the second step, we must contemplate upon that knowledge. This is called *mananam*. The third and final step is *nididhyāsanam*, which means to decide with the intellect in accordance with that knowledge.

But if the first step is messed up—if the knowledge we hear is itself defective—then the second and third steps only compound the mess. As a result, it is vitally important that the source of our knowledge must be reliable. What is that perfect source?

According to the Vedic scriptures, knowledge originated by human beings is subject to four kinds of defects: 1) *Karṇāpāṭava*, 2) *Bhram,* 3) *Pramāda,* and 4) *Vipralipsā.* Let's look at them closely.

### 1. *Karṇāpāṭava* (limited senses or lack of experience)

We humans have five knowledge-acquiring senses—eyes, ears, nose, tongue, and skin (sense of touch). These senses work only within a limited range of perception. For example, the human eye cannot see objects that are too small. To increase the range, we use microscopes, and yet atomic movement remains obscure. That is why particles like the Higgs-Boson must be assumed to exist based on estimation, for they cannot be proven by visual evidence.

2. ***Bhram*** **(illusion)**

Humans are subject to two kinds of illusions. The first is to confuse one entity for another. For example, we confuse a bronze chain for a gold chain. We confuse the body with the self. Likewise, we assume that the temporary things of the world will permanently remain with us.

The second kind of illusion is to perceive an entity where none exists. For example, the mirage in the desert creates a perception of water though there is none. Similarly, we believe the objects of our senses will give us happiness, and we keep running after the illusion.

3. ***Pramāda*** **(mistakes)**

Sometimes, we inadvertently make mistakes. As the saying goes, 'To err is human.' For example, doctors intend to prescribe one medicine, but inadvertently write another in the patient's slip. Pharmacists make errors in dispensing medicines. In the same way, mistakes are made in the writing of computer programs, books, etc.

4. ***Vipralipsā*** **(propensity to cheat)**

This is the tendency to make false claims with the intention of cheating others or wanting them to perceive us as 'good'. Spouses cheat each other over small and large matters. Even learned scientists announce fake results of experiments to garner prestige.

This defect is akin to hypocrisy, which is the tendency to hide one's faults and portray non-existent virtues.

These four defects exist in all human beings. Hence, if we look to humans to share their wisdom, it cannot be flawless. Instead, if we want knowledge free from these four kinds of imperfections, then we must find a perfect source.

Such a flawless source of knowledge are the Vedas. The reason they are so highly respected is that they are *apauruṣheya*, meaning, not created by a human. They were manifested by God Himself at the beginning of creation. Thus, they contain knowledge that is perfect. We observe in the world how scientific theories keep superseding each other every few decades. But the spiritual principles of Vedic scriptures are the same after thousands of years. Consequently, the *Manu Smṛiti* states:

*bhūtaṁ bhavyaṁ bhaviṣhyaṁ cha sarvaṁ vedāt prasidhyati*
(verse 12.97)

'The ultimate authority for determining the veracity of any spiritual principle are the Vedas.'

The same Vedic knowledge was further explained and elaborated by God-realized saints in the various Vedic scriptures. When we create beliefs based upon these two perfect sources—God-realized saints and Vedic scripture—such beliefs are called *shraddha*. Jagadguru Shankaracharya explained its meaning:

*guru vedānta vākyeṣhu dṛiṛho viśhvāsaḥ śhraddhā*

'*Shraddha* is firm belief in the words of the Vedic texts and the guru.'

Interestingly, *shraddha* is contagious—we can catch it from the saints who are endowed with it. This means that if one personality is endowed with *shraddha*, and we associate with such a person, we also develop similar faith in the scriptures and the saints. Sage Tulsidas states:

*eka gharī ādhī gharī ādhī meṅ puni ādha*
*tulasī saṅgata sādhu kī koṭī kaṭe aparādha*

'Association with genuine saints is such a benediction that, even in a fraction of a moment, it can free us from sins.' Why? Because it leads to the development of faith in the divine knowledge.

**In conclusion, the way to develop good beliefs, or *shraddha*, is to associate with the scriptures and the guru.** And the process for it is called satsang, which literally means 'that association which takes our mind to the Truth.' The Shreemad Bhagavatam explains:

*satāṁ prasaṅgān mama vīrya-saṁvido,*
*bhavanti hṛit-karṇa-rasāyanāḥ kathāḥ*
*taj-joṣhaṇād āśhv apavarga-vartmani,*
*śhraddhā ratir bhaktir anukramiṣhyati* (3.25.25)

This verse states that when we associate with saintly personalities, we hear divine wisdom from them, which is like nectar to our ears. From such hearing, first faith develops, next attachment to God, and then gradually divine love manifests in the heart.

**The aim of this book is to sow seeds of good beliefs in your intellect.** In it, I have taken spiritual principles from the Vedic scriptures and sages, and then explained that same wisdom with modern examples and real-life stories, to help you connect with it.

The most vital belief we will ever establish in our life is about happiness. Our opinion about how we can become happy will determine our values, morals, attitudes, goals, and much more. Therefore, let us discuss the topic of happiness next.

## Key Takeaways

- Beyond willpower is why-power. It is the impetus that arises when we are deeply motivated.
- Willpower is our ability to control our mind, while why-power comes from the beliefs we hold in our intellect. The Bhagavad Gita asks us to tap into both for success.
- Beliefs are the biggest force within our personality because our subconscious assumes them to be true, irrespective of the facts.
- For better or for worse, the trajectory of our life is determined by our beliefs.
- Bad beliefs are based upon defective knowledge. Nothing can ruin our life more than them.
- Good beliefs must be based on a trustworthy source of knowledge.
- Knowledge created by humans is subject to four kinds of defects. To get infallible knowledge we must approach the Vedic scriptures and the saints.
- To transform knowledge into beliefs, we must follow the three-step process of *śhravaṇ-manan-nididhyāsan*, or hearing-contemplation-faith.

# 4

# The Law of Happiness

This fourth chapter of the book is about happiness, which is an enormously profound topic. I must caution you that it will be the most philosophical chapter in the book. The conclusion will be surprisingly simple and immensely valuable. But to reach it, we will sequentially proceed through a series of logical arguments. Do peruse through them, as it will definitely be worth your while.

## We All Are Searching for Happiness

All of us are looking to be happy. We hold differing views regarding where it lies, but our goal is the same. One person believes happiness is found in the company of friends, while another is convinced that it is reached by leaving society and residing in the Himalayas. Though these two hold diametrically opposite ideas, yet both are looking for the same thing—joy, bliss, peace, *anand, mazā, sukh, lutf.* These are all various names for the same entity.

Approximately 2,500 years ago, Aristotle realized this commonality in our lives and suggested: 'Happiness is the meaning and the purpose of life, the whole aim and end of human existence.' Aristotle may have been intrigued to know that 2,500 years before him, the Vedas declared the same truth more emphatically:

*prayojanamanuddiśhya mando 'pi na pravartate*

'Not even a lunatic does anything without a motive; and the one motive of all of us is happiness.' Every action we take is either in search of it or an interim step towards it.

*For example, let us say a farmer is working in his field. Why is he toiling hard? So that he can get a good harvest. Why does he want abundant harvest? So that he can sell the grain for a good sum of money. Why does he want lots of money? So that he can purchase a comfortable home and a nice car. Why does he want these luxurious facilities? So that he can get a good wife and raise a loving family. Why does he want a good family life? So that he can be happy.*

**Ultimately, we all want happiness, and if we seem to want anything else, it is because we believe it will bring us happiness.** If people become convinced that they cannot get happiness in their life, they even go to the extent of committing suicide. 'If that boy had married me, I would have been happy. He went and married another girl. Now I can never get joy. So, let me put an end to my life.'

Look at the advertisements everywhere around us. They all promise to make us happy in different ways. Though our goal is the same, we differ in our ways to attain it. This leads to the variety that we see in the world.

## Four Kinds of People in the World

When it comes to the ways in which we seek happiness, we can be classified into one of the four categories:

> *eke satpuruṣhāḥ parārthaghaṭakāḥ svārthaṁ parityajya ye*
> *sāmānyāstu parārthamudyamabhṛitaḥ svārthāvirodhena ye*
> *te 'mī mānuṣharākṣhasāḥ parahitaṁ svārthāya nighnanti ye*
> *ye tu ghnanti nirarthakaṁ parahitaṁ te ke na jānīmahe*
> (*Nīti Shatak* 75)

Sage Bhartrihari states in this verse that human beings are of the following types:

- The first kind of people are those who work to help others without any selfish motive. Says Bhartrihari, 'These are the saintly personalities.'
- The second type are those who work to fulfil their self-interest, but also keep in mind not to harm the interests of others. Says Bhartrihari, 'These are the ordinary human beings.'
- The third kind are those who do not hesitate to hurt the interests of others, while fulfilling their own. Says Bhartrihari, 'These are the demonic-natured ones.'
- In the last category are those who work to hurt others, even though they hurt themselves as well in the process. Says Bhartrihari, 'They are so evil that I have no name for them.'

From this analysis, it seems that two types of people do not seek their own happiness: 1) The saintly natured who help others without any self-interest, 2) Extremely evil people who hurt others without reason.

No, not really! Even these two types of people do have a selfish goal. What is it? The Ramayan states:

*santa hṛidaya navanīta samānā,*
*kahā kavinha pari kahai na jānā*

The verse implies that the heart of saintly people is so soft that they become sad on seeing others suffer, while they are happy on seeing others rejoice. Hence, even at the cost of personal loss, they help others, since it makes them feel good.

Now let us look at the wicked people. Again, the Ramayan states:

*kāhū kī jauñ sunahiṅ baṛāī, svāsa lehiṅ janū jūṛī āī*
*jo kāhū kai dekhahiṅ vipatī, sukhī bhae mānahuñ jaga nṛipatī*

'Evil people feel blissful on seeing others in plight, and miserable on seeing them prosper. Thus, they do not hesitate to plunder others even at the cost of hurting their own self, since it brings them joy.'

We see that even these two categories of people are trying to be happy. Thus, we can conclude that whatever be our way of trying to arrive at it, everyone's eventual goal is happiness.

Now, what is the difficulty in achieving bliss?

## The Paradox of Happiness

The mystery is that we all strive for bliss, and yet, like the beautiful rainbow in the horizon, we never reach it. In fact, the more we pursue happiness, the more miserable we seem to become. If we simply look around us, this is precisely what we will observe.

More than 70 years have gone by since India gained independence. In this period, the average household income has increased by 700 per cent. This is real income I am talking about—after discounting for inflation. That real income has increased seven-fold in seven decades. But do you hear the good news that people in India are much happier today?

Quite the reverse. During this period, the number of *crorepatis* in the country has multiplied a hundred-fold. However, from the data that I could gather and estimate, the number of people saying they are happy has halved; the teen suicide rate has tripled; the depression rate has quadrupled; and the divorce rate has increased five times. (Even after such a rapid increase, the divorce rate in India is still the lowest in the world. Regrettably, we are catching up with the other countries rapidly.)

What is the problem here? We all are running for fulfilment but finding the opposite. This was the conundrum that Mahatma Vidur put before Maitreya Rishi:

*sukhāya karmāṇi karoti loke*
*na taiḥ sukhaṁ vānyadupāramaṁ vā*
(Shreemad Bhagavatam 3.5.2)

'Everyone in the world tries to be happy. Instead, why do they beget suffering?' I am reminded of an anecdote:

*A man was on his first visit to a home for the mentally challenged. The warden of the institution was taking him around. They came across an inmate who was sitting in his chamber, and incessantly repeating, 'Laila ... Laila ... Laila ...'*

*'Why is he uttering the word "Laila" like a parrot?' asked the surprised visitor.*

*'He loved a girl called Laila,' responded the warden. 'She went and married someone else. That made him lose his mental balance, and now he keeps chanting her name.'*

*Subsequently, they came across another inmate who was also sitting in his chamber, and chanting, 'Laila ... Laila ... Laila ...'*

*Astonished, the visitor asked, 'How come he is also uttering the same lady's name? Did she have many lovers?'*

*'No,' replied the warden. 'He is the man who married Laila. He also went mad.'*

The joke is not a dig at wives. To balance it out, let me relate one about husbands as well.

*A husband woke up in the morning and spoke to his wife with great concern for her well-being, 'My dear! Were you having horrid dreams at night? You were constantly saying nasty things about me.'*

*'I was not dreaming,' responded the wife. 'I was wide awake.'*

Jokes apart, let us analyse what is happening here. The quest to derive happiness from anything involves three stages: 1) **Before** the object, person, or position is attained, 2) **While** we have our cherished object, person, or position, and 3) **After** that desired object, person, or position is lost. Each of these stages has its associated distress.

For example, suppose a citizen wishes to become the mayor of her city. The stages in getting to her cherished happiness are:

1. ***Before becoming mayor***

To fulfil her desire, she prioritizes community interaction at the cost of quality time with her family. She seeks social gatherings where she can give speeches. She pretends to be pally with other political bigwigs in the community. Every statement she makes is closely scrutinized by opponents, who wait to tear it apart in case of any small error.

Consequently, the peace of mind she enjoyed earlier is gone. In striving to get her cherished position, she experiences distress.

2. ***While she is mayor***

Now suppose that eventually, she wins the elections. She does experience joy for a little while. But it is ephemeral, and soon she starts worrying about protecting the goodwill she has gathered. The opposition constantly tries to malign her and ruin her public image.

In this way, after getting her cherished position, she has two distresses to deal with. The first is the effort to maintain her post. And the second is the apprehension of losing it in the future.

3. ***After she loses the mayorship***

Finally, suppose she completes her term and stands for re-election, but loses this time. Now, she misses her previous popularity and power and feels awfully miserable.

This is the distress we experience when the object, person, or position we were relishing is separated from us.

From the above we see that **in striving for happiness anywhere, there are three stages—before getting the object, after we have it, and when it is separated from us. Each of these stages is associated with distress.** Then why are we striving so hard? We believe that we are not blissful yet, but our efforts will bring us joy in the future. Consequently, let us continue the logical analysis a little further.

## The Illusion of Future Happiness

Most people think they do not have joy presently, but they hope to get it in the future. Their present possessions are not enough to make them happy. If only they could possess more, or reach the next higher class, they would certainly find fulfilment.

The poor think if only they can become millionaires, everything will be all right. But if you ask the millionaires whether they are happy, they will say that a million is not enough. They need a billion to be happy. Now enquire from the billionaires whether they are happy, and they will tell you they cannot sleep until they take sleeping pills.

What is happening here is an ever-receding illusion of happiness. This can be compared to a mirage in the desert. Due to reflection of the sunrays on the hot desert sand, the deer sees an illusion of water ahead. It runs to quench its thirst, but more the deer moves towards it, the more the illusion recedes. In the same manner, we too feel that if we can enhance our material possessions, we will be happy, but the chase never ends.

In developing countries, people believe if they could live in America, it would be like paradise. Hence, visas for the US are so eagerly sought. However, while travelling around the US, I often ask Indians living there, 'People in India think that since you live in the land of plenty, you must be incredibly happy. Are they correct in thinking so?'

The answer I most often get is, 'Swamiji, from far it seemed that way to us. But after living here, we realize that our experience of happiness is just the same.'

Still, those in India will not agree. 'How can they not be happy living in America, in the midst of so many opportunities and opulence?'

But the same illusion of distant happiness continues in the US as well.

*Once I was giving a lecture in Tampa, Florida. On the last day of the weeklong programme, a lady asked me, 'Swamiji, where are you going from here?'*

*'New York,' I replied.*

*She became all goggle-eyed. 'New York!' she exclaimed, as if it were the land of pleasure.*

*Next, in New York, I asked my audience, 'This is what the rest of America thinks of you all—that you live in the paradise of pleasure. Are they right in thinking so?'*

*I did not need a reply. Their sullen faces told it all. New York reminds me so much of Mumbai. When New Yorkers travel in the local metro or try to find parking space in Manhattan, all pleasure gets squeezed dry. Nevertheless, the rest of America is convinced that it is Shangri La.*

As the saying goes in English: 'The grass is always greener on the other side of the fence.' Everyone is thinking, 'I am not happy; the other person must be happy.' However, **the Vedas inform us that the various levels of material happiness look to be one higher than the previous. But when we reach the next level, we soon become discontent and wish to go to the subsequent level.**

A factory worker wants to be the foreman. The foreman is seeking to be a plant manager. The plant manager wishes to be chief of production. But the irony is that the chief of production is equally dissatisfied and hankers to be chief executive.

*chakradharo 'pi suratvaṁ suratvalābhe sakalasurapatitvam*
*bhavituṁ surapatirūrdhvagatitvaṁ tathāpi nanivartate tṛiṣhṇā*

(*Garuḍ Purāṇ*)

This verse states that a king wishes to be emperor of the world; the emperor seeks to be a celestial god; the celestial *devata* wishes to be Indra, the king of the celestial abodes; Indra desires the post of Brahma. There is never any end to desires.

The fact is that these categories only appear to be different, but the experience of happiness is just the same. If this is true, then why can we not find happiness despite our best efforts? What is the mistake we are making?

## Why Happiness Evades Us

Sigmund Freud is revered as the father of psychoanalysis. All of us have heard his name. But what few people know is that despite all his theorizations about the mind, Freud was a terribly unhappy person. In his book, *Civilization and Its Discontents*, he wrote: 'What good to us is a long life if it is difficult and barren of joys, and if it is so full of misery that we can only welcome death as a deliverer?'

This is the confounding riddle of happiness. Everyone is running for it, but nobody is reaching it. Let us analyse this puzzle a little more philosophically. The Mahabharat states:

*prakṣhālanāddhi paṅkasya dūrād asparśhanaṁ varam*

This verse states that it is better to not get your feet dirty in the first place than asking for water to clean them. Similarly, we make desires for happiness, but these very desires become the cause of our unhappiness. We would be better off without creating them.

The example below illustrates how our own desires for happiness bring us misery.

*Let us say, Ramesh and Dinesh are two roommates in a hostel. Ten o'clock at night, Ramesh creates a desire, 'I need to smoke a cigarette to be happy.'*

*Dinesh ticked him off, 'It is already bedtime. What is the need for a cigarette? Forget it and go to sleep.'*

*Dinesh retired for the night, but Ramesh could not rest. The desire for cigarettes continued to agitate him to no end. He went to the hostel store, but it was already closed. He tried the college shop, but it was also closed. So, he rode his motorcycle to the shop in front of the campus main gate. He found it open, but that night, it was out of cigarettes. Searching further, he finally got his favourite Charminar brand at a nearby marketplace. He purchased a pack and returned to his hostel. There he smoked it, relishing every puff of it. Relieved, he went off to sleep.*

*Next morning, Dinesh asked, 'Ramesh, what time did you sleep last night?'*

*'Twelve o'clock.'*

*'What, you stayed up till midnight? Don't tell me you were agitated from ten o'clock for two hours! And then, at twelve you reached where you were at ten o'clock.'*

*Ramesh was astonished by his friend's observation. 'What do you mean? How can you say that I reached at twelve o'clock where I was at ten o'clock?'*

*Dinesh explained to him, 'Look, at ten o'clock you did not have any desire for cigarettes; you were peaceful. Then you created a desire within yourself. It agitated you. For two hours, you struggled to fulfil it. And when it was satiated, where did you reach? At the same place where you were two hours earlier–free from the desire for cigarettes. I, on the other hand, did not create any desire for relishing a puff of Charminar. I went to sleep peacefully at ten o'clock itself.'*

**We make desires because we want joy. But the very same desires become the cause of our misery. And the goal of happiness remains as distant as before.**

Why is happiness so evasive? The question is exceedingly profound. But the answer is equally simple. **We are searching for happiness in the wrong place. If we look for something where it is not present, our chances of finding it will always be zero.**

*Kaka Hathrasi, the Hindi humour poet, was looking for something under the lamppost in front of his home. Seeing him desperately searching, his neighbour asked, 'Kaka, what is it that you have lost?'*

*'My keys,' replied Kaka.*

*'Where did you lose them?' questioned his neighbour.*

*'They fell on my living room floor,' responded Kaka.*

*'But Kaka, if they fell in your living room, then why are you searching for them here?'*

*'Because there is no light in the living room,' Kaka answered.*

Kaka was enacting a satire on human nature. Like his search for keys under the lamppost, we too are looking for happiness in the wrong place. Though we are divine spiritual beings, we hope to find satiation in material objects. Through the five physical senses we offer sensory happiness to the soul. No matter what pleasure we savour, our soul from within gives the decision, 'This does not satisfy me; I am still thirsty for real joy. Give me divine bliss.'

If material pleasure cannot fulfil us, then what kind of happiness will?

## The Nature of True Happiness

Let us now understand the nature of bliss that our soul seeks. It must possess three characteristics: *sat-chit-anand.* These are the three traits of divine bliss.

- *Sat* implies that it is everlasting,
- *Chit* implies that it is ever fresh, and
- *Anand* implies that it is infinite.

*Sat-chit-anand* is the nature of true bliss. Let us look at each in detail.

1. ***Our soul wants bliss that lasts forever.***

Happiness that comes and goes cannot satisfy us. Let us say, someone partied yesterday and had great fun. But today he fell sick and got bored staying at home. As you can see, yesterday's happiness went away today. Can such bliss that comes for a day and then goes away fulfil us permanently? Absolutely not! That is the problem with the 'high' people get from consuming alcohol. It is short-lived and followed by a 'hangover' the next morning.

2. ***Our soul seeks bliss that is ever fresh.***

Happiness that keeps fading will not satisfy us. We hear a good poem and get a kick out of it. Hear it again and the pleasure is less. Hear it ten times, and it becomes like a punishment. It is the same poem, but the joy from it keeps reducing. Is it possible for such happiness to always fulfil us?

3. ***Our soul desires bliss that is infinite.***

Happiness that is limited does not satisfy. Someone becomes a Member of Parliament and feels happy. But the pleasure is finite, and so a little while later, he sees a minister, and thinks, 'O my God, she is a cabinet minister, while I am only Member of Parliament.' In other words, no matter what happiness we get, if we find a class above it, we again become unhappy. Our soul is unwilling to be satisfied with finite happiness.

**All of us want happiness that is permanent, ever fresh, and infinite. Since the mundane pleasures of the world do not fulfil these parameters, we remain discontented.**

The unlimited bliss we are looking for is in God. He is referred to in the Vedas as *sat-chit-anand.* I am quoting below a few of the thousands of verses in the scriptures where the Supreme is referred to by these names:

*satyaṁ vijñānaṁ ānandaṁ brahma*
(*Bṛihadāraṇyak Upaniṣhad* 3.9.28)

*satyaṁ jñānamanantaṁ brahma*
(*Taittirīya Upaniṣhad* 2.1.2)

*ānandamayo 'bhyāsāt* (*Brahma Sūtra* 1.1.12)

*satya jñānāntānanda mātraika rasa mūrtayaḥ*
(Shreemad Bhagavatam 10.13.54)

*ānanda mātra kara pāda mukhodarādī* (*Padma Purāṇ*)

*ānanda sindhu madhya tava vāsā* (Ramayan)

The divine bliss of God is eternal, ever fresh, and infinite. And He is seated within us. Hence, **we do not need to physically go to any place to reach happiness. We only need to go within ourselves.**

The question that arises now is, how will we go within ourselves to find the source of happiness? This is an important topic so let's take it up next.

## The Way to Be Truly Happy

The reservoir of infinite bliss resides in us, yet we look for it in external objects. This is like running to reach some paradise in a distant land but missing the flower garden right outside our home. Saint Kabir makes fun of this:

*pānī bicha mīna piyāsī, mohi suni suni āvata hāsī*

'The fish is in the water and yet thirsty. How ridiculous! But that is exactly what human beings do.' People spend all their energy trying to reach some future destination of happiness. In the meantime, life passes by in unhappiness. We are like the *kastūrī* deer.

*The kastūrī deer has a very curious behaviour. The sac of musk inside the deer has such a strong aroma that it spreads for miles around. The deer runs hither and thither, in the forest, hoping to reach the wonderful scent. It does not realize that the source of the aroma is within itself.*

The ocean of happiness, the Supreme Divinity, is sitting inside us. Hence, the way to be happy is to go closer to God. And how do we do that? The Vedas prescribe that **the purer we become, the closer we get to God.**

This means that the path to true happiness is to become a better person. Plain and simple answer. Sometimes we miss the truth merely because it is so simple, while we look for it in complexities. Now, let me state the fourth divine law:

## The Law of Happiness

*True happiness comes by growing from within to become a better person.*

Intuitively, you knew this law all the while, is it not? The only problem was that nobody ever told it to you so straight. Today, I am simply confirming what your inner being always knew—that the way to be happier is not by accumulating possessions, but by becoming a better person.

Unfortunately, all our life we prioritize a hundred tasks over and above the task of working upon ourselves. Think about it. How much time in a year do we allocate to self-improvement?

Our focus is upon doing … doing … doing, and in the process, we neglect being … being … being. **The sequence for success is that 'being' must precede 'doing'. We must be genuinely good before we can truly do something worthwhile.**

Presently, our sequence is the reverse. We focus on achieving great works. But we neglect the foundation for it, which is becoming better people ourselves. Instead, if we could shift the focus on growing from within, we would become more successful in our external works as well.

Let us understand this more deeply.

### Grow from Within to Succeed in Life

*Every year, as a part of my US tour, I conduct a weeklong 'Life Transformation Program', or LTP, in twenty different cities, including*

*Denver, Colorado. The Rocky Mountains nearby are exceptionally beautiful, and we spend a morning atop the panoramic peaks.*

*On one such occasion, we had gone up Pikes Peak, which at 14,000 feet is the highest summit of the southern Front Range. On the way back, while yet on the mountainside, we had stopped for a break, and I decided to explore the surroundings.*

*I walked over a hillock and, as far as I could see, there were rocks and dry mud covers. Then suddenly my eyes fell on a beautiful flower blossoming in the middle of nowhere. In that arid environment, it was growing with all its splendour. It seemed to be challenging the barrenness of the land with its colourful and exquisite presence.*

The flower had bloomed wherever its seed happened to fall. This got me thinking, 'Why can we not thrive wherever we are in life?' People keep changing their jobs, cars, homes, friends, and even life partners. But they never think of changing themselves.

This is where our perspective differs from God's perspective. **We are more interested in changing our environment, while God is more interested in changing us.** In fact, difficult circumstances are given to us for the same purpose—to make us grow. Just as a carpenter uses sandpaper to smoothen rough edges, the Universe provides us with hardships that compel us to evolve.

The flower in that arid hillside also had its challenges. There was lack of water, wild animals, dry winds, and extreme cold. And yet it had managed to blossom. Why cannot human beings do the same? People fret and fume about the externals in their life—their marriage, their work environment, their neighbourhood, and so on. In the process, they forget the purpose of life, which is to become a better person. When we take care of this one fundamental aspect, external success will naturally follow.

Blaise Pascal was a famous French mathematician, physicist, and philosopher. Someone said to him, 'If I had your brains, I would be a better person.' Pascal replied, 'Be a better person and you will have my brains.'

**We must undoubtedly work hard at our job, but we should work harder upon ourselves. Always remember that our inner growth is the foundation of outer success.**

*You may have heard of Bonsai. It is a Japanese art form using cultivation techniques to produce small trees in containers. I would not recommend it to anyone; it hurts to see the huge trees growing as little dwarfs. But the point to ponder is, how did the giant oak grown in bonsai remain so stunted? The reason was that the roots did not have space to grow. Since they remained tiny, the tree could not manifest even a fraction of its potential.*

Similarly, what we do in life is limited by how good we are from within. If we wish to do more, we must prioritize self-improvement. Then, as we become better, we will naturally be motivated to do the best we can do. And when we try to do our finest at work, we will discover it requires us to improve ourselves even further. In this way, with proper understanding, 'being' and 'doing' feed each other.

People ask me whether they should be ambitious to do well at work. I respond that they must certainly be ambitious at work, but in a meaningful and purposeful way, because in the process, they will realize they must also grow from within. Then, by 'being good' and 'doing good', they will 'feel good'—they will experience inner satisfaction. This is the happiness which is beyond the objects of the senses. It arises from within and cannot be snatched away by anyone or anything because is not dependent upon external objects or circumstances.

To conclude our discussion on happiness, the way to divine bliss is to try and be the best we can be and do the best that we can do. As a result, we will experience the happiness that our soul is seeking.

This brings up the next question. How can we become better people? We shall discuss it in the next chapter.

## Key Takeaways

- Ultimately, we all want happiness, and if we seem to want anything else, it is because we believe it will bring us happiness.
- The various levels of material happiness look to be one higher than the previous. But when we reach the next level, we soon become discontented and wish to go to the subsequent level.
- We are searching for happiness in the wrong place. True happiness comes by growing from within to become a better person.
- We do not need to go anywhere physically to reach happiness. We only need to go within ourselves.
- We are more interested in changing our environment, while God is more interested in changing us.
- The sequence for success is that 'being' must precede 'doing'. We must be genuinely good before we can truly do something worthwhile.

# 5

# The Law of Sublimation

WHAT DOES it mean to improve ourselves? Do we become better by donning stylish clothes and lavish make-up? Or are we improved when we live in posh colonies and drive luxury cars? Or else is inner progress a manifestation of our position and popularity in society?

The truth is that none of these are a measurement of our betterment. Then what is? Deterioration and betterment are determined by the state of our mind. If the mind is filled with mundane thoughts, then despite external adornments, we are at the mundane level. And if the mind harbours noble emotions, then we are elevated, no matter how meagre our apparel, finances, and social status.

## We Are Where Our Mind Is

In teamwork, there is a saying, 'You are only as strong as your weakest link.' Our weakest link is the unconquered mind. Until we control and purify it, the level of our consciousness will remain anchored to the quality of our mind.

We learn from the Vedic scriptures that the mind is the cause of bondage:

*chetaḥ khalvasya bandhāya muktaye cātmano matam*
*guṇeṣhu saktaṁ bandhāya rataṁ vā puṁsi muktaye*

(Shreemad Bhagavatam 3.25.15)

'Bondage and liberation are determined by the state of the mind. If the mind is attached to the three gunas, there is bondage; and if it is absorbed in the Supreme, it results in liberation.'

From the spiritual perspective, it is not our physical location, but our mental situation, that determines our ultimate destination. The Puranas relate a story about this.

*Tavrit and Suvrit were two brothers. They started off from their home to listen to the Bhagavad kathā at the temple, which was an hour away.*

*On the way, they ran into a terrible storm. To save themselves from the heavy downpour, they ran into the only building nearby. Inside, they were shocked to discover that they had unknowingly entered a brothel. Ladies of the night were dancing to lewd music, while men of loose morals sat around consuming liquor.*

*Tavrit was appalled. 'How awful! I cannot stay in this place for another minute. Come on, Suvrit. Let's leave this very moment.'*

*Suvrit, in contrast, was nonchalant about it. 'Dear brother, if we go out, we will get drenched. Let us stay here until the rain stops. We can look the other way; we do not have to look at the dance.'*

*'What? Your mind is already polluted!' Tavrit berated. 'That is why you are making excuses to remain in this building of sin.' He stomped out, and braving the rain, reached the temple, where panditji was relating the Bhagavad kathā.*

*There, sitting in the audience, Tavrit started regretting, 'How boring this is! I made a big mistake. Suvrit must be really enjoying life watching the* mujrā. *I should have remained there too.'*

*Conversely, waiting in the house of ill-repute, Suvrit started bemoaning, 'What a big blunder I made by staying here! My body is not made of salt that it would have dissolved in the rain. Look at Tavrit. He is so pious; he is hearing the sacred episodes of the Bhagavatam.'*

*When the downpour ended, both brothers came out of their respective buildings and began walking towards each other. The moment they met, lightening fell, and both suffered a spot death.*

*The messengers from hell, Yamdoots, came to take Tavrit. 'You have gotten my name wrong,' he shrieked. 'You should be taking Suvrit. He was sitting at the* mujrā *while I was attending the Bhagavad kathā.'*

*The Yamdoots responded, 'We have the names right. We have been asked to take you, Tavrit. You were physically in the temple, but mentally you were in the brothel. On the other hand, your brother, Suvrit was physically in the building of sin, but mentally he was at the temple.'*

Hence, the Hindi saying states: *jahāṅ mana vahāṅ hama*. Veritably, we are where our mind is. John Milton expressed the same idea in his classic work, *Paradise Lost*: 'The mind is its own place, and in itself can make a heaven of hell, a hell of heaven.'

**Self-improvement, therefore, requires working on uplifting our mind and its thoughts.** Next, let us understand what pulls our mind down, and how it can be enriched.

## The Nexus of Unwholesome Thoughts

The mind can be compared to a subtle machine fitted within. One of its primary functions is to generate thoughts. And these thoughts in turn create the emotions of happiness and distress. Impure and unwholesome thoughts cause us misery, while noble and loving thoughts make us joyful.

You can literally know if a thought is holy or unholy by the feeling it generates. Since we all want to be happy, and our internal mechanism is uncomfortable with impure thoughts, we wish to get rid of them. The Bhagavad Gita identifies the three most harmful kinds of thoughts and refers to them as pathways to the nether regions.

*tri-vidhaṁ narakasyedaṁ dvāraṁ nāśhanam ātmanaḥ*
*kāmaḥ krodhas tathā lobhas tasmād etat trayaṁ tyajet*

(Bhagavad Gita 16.21)

'There are three gates leading to the hell of self-destruction for the soul—desire, anger, and greed. Therefore, abandon all three.'

Desire is the primary culprit in this triad. It leads to contemplation of the object of our desire which in turn increases our attachment. Greater attachment leads to greater desire. And that means further contemplation, which means even further desire. In this way, layer after layer of desire and attachment keep shrouding our mind.

What happens when we try to fulfil desire? The result is greed for even more. Conversely, what happens when desire is thwarted? It gives rise to anger.

This is the unholy nexus—contemplation, attachment, desire, anger, greed—that contaminates and defiles our mind. The defilement creates a sense of inner discomfort. To overcome the inner unpleasantness, we must try to improve ourselves. In this manner, the battle ensues within our own personality.

Now, we have two natures at work within us. One is our lower nature consisting of harmful attachments and unholy desires. But we also have a higher nature that dislikes our lower impulses. This is why we struggle to rise above our frailties by giving up unholy desires and undignified attachments.

Only problem here is that suppression has the reverse effect.

## The Ironic Process Theory

By now we have understood the need to eliminate impure thoughts—desire, greed, anger, and attachment. The difficulty arises when our efforts create opposite results.

*The White Bear experiment is famous in psychological circles. It was first performed in laboratory settings in 1987 by Daniel Wegner, a social psychology professor at Harvard University. One group of people was instructed, 'Force your mind not to think of a white bear during the next twenty-four hours.' The other group was told, 'Note how many times you think of a white bear during the next twenty-four hours.'*

*Both groups were given counters to keep track of the number of times the thought of a white bear came to them. The results were surprising. The group that had been forbidden from thinking of a white bear was doing so more often.*

*The result was ironically opposite to the instructions.*

This made Wegner postulate the **Ironic Process Theory. It states that trying to suppress undesirable thoughts does not work; rather, it backfires with more of the same.**

Consider the following examples:

- You have an important engagement next morning, so you go to bed early with thoughts of a good night's rest. But what happens is quite the reverse; you discover you are wide awake.
- A dieter decides to keep off certain foods, but he discovers that the forbidden foods are the ones repeatedly coming to mind.
- A candidate goes for a job interview. She so desperately wants to make a good impression on the interviewer. But during the interview she finds herself blurting out the very things she had planned not to mention.
- You are bringing a tray of cups filled with tea for your guests, with one thought in your mind—the tea should not spill. But ironically you find yourself making the very mistake you were anxious to avoid.

In all these cases, we find that the results are opposite of our intentions.

Wegner explained the reason for this. He said that when we plan not to think of something, our mind splits into two parts—the operator and the monitor. The operator guides, 'Do not think of it. Do not think of it.' The other half, the monitor, keeps scanning, 'Am I thinking of it? Am I thinking of it?'

The monitor works just a shade away from our conscious awareness. It continuously processes the very thought we did not want. The problem arises if the monitor is energized while the operator is tired. The monitor then begins to dominate, and the very thought we wished to avoid starts pinging upon our mind.

Here is a humorous example of the Ironic Process Theory.

*Some people believe that watching the moon is very inauspicious on one night of the year. This is the fourth night of the* Śhukla Paksh *(waxing moon) of the month of* Bhādra *in the Hindu calendar. Now look at the effect of the belief.*

*On a normal night, people never bother to look at the moon unless it comes before them. But, if you get out of your home thinking, 'Tonight is the* chaturthī *(fourth night) of* Śhukla Paksh *of* Bhādra. *I must not look at the moon ... I must not look at the moon ...' the consequence will be that from some corner of your eye, you will end up seeing the moon, because the thought was constantly being processed in your subconscious.*

This contradictory result of suppression creates great challenges in our efforts of mind management.

## The Problem in Restraining the Mind

Within us are harmful thoughts of desire, greed, anger, hatred, and bitterness. We naturally wish to eradicate them. In Vedic terminology, these are called *mānas rog* (mental afflictions). The phenomenon of ironic effects applies to them as well.

Suppose a relative hurt you emotionally, and you wish to give up bitterness towards him or her. So, you tell yourself, 'I must give up resentment.' Towards whom? 'Towards my relative.' Now every time you think of giving it up, you find the target of your bitterness coming to your mind. This only increases the resentful thoughts.

Similarly, suppose you learn from a spiritual lecture that attachment is harmful. Hence, you resolve, 'I will give up attachment.' Whom am I attached to? 'My son.' Now every time you think of giving up affection, you discover the very object of your affection pinging upon your mind. This only results in deepening your attachment even further.

The mind's nature is to keep thinking. If you try to make your mind thoughtless, you will realize it is extremely difficult. The story below illustrates this concept.

*Milarepa was a Buddhist monk, who lived in Tibet during the fifteenth century AD. He is considered one of the most famous yogis and siddhas in Vajrayana Buddhism. He used to reside in a cave on a hill, by the village of Pelgyeling Gompa.*

*Once, a rumour spread in the village that Milarepa possessed a siddha mantra. A villager came to him and said, 'O sage, please give me your siddha mantra, so I may also develop miraculous abilities.'*

*Milarepa responded, 'The mantra is Om. It will result in siddhis if you fulfil a condition. Do not bring monkeys to your mind or all your chanting will be futile.'*

*The villager returned, delighted that he had a siddha mantra. He began chanting, 'Om, Om, Om, ...' and alongside kept contemplating, 'I must not think of monkeys.' But the more he tried not to remember, the more thoughts of monkeys came to his mind.*

*Finally, he returned to Milarepa, and said, 'O sage, please take back your siddha mantra. Give it to me in my next life, but do not tell me that I should not think of monkeys or I will definitely think of them.'*

This story highlights that **as a spiritual practice, the goal of stopping the mind from thinking is a difficult one.** There is a better alternative to it.

## Dovetail Your Mind Towards God

The path of bhakti tells us not to stop the thinking process; rather, to divert it towards God. Compare it with riding a bicycle. If you press the brakes, then retaining balance will be impossible. You will fall either to the left or to the right. But instead, if you turn the handle sideways, the forward movement will easily stop.

**In bhakti, we dovetail our mind towards the Divine. Consequently, detrimental material desires and attachments are replaced by divine love for God.** Since the Supreme Divine Personality is all-pure, slowly the mind too gets purified and develops sublime qualities. This is the message of the Bhagavad Gita:

*māṁ cha yo 'vyabhichāreṇa bhakti-yogena sevate*
*sa guṇān samatītyaitān brahma-bhūyāya kalpate* (14.26)

'Those who absorb their minds in Me, with unadulterated devotion, rise above the three modes of material nature and attain the Supreme Brahman.'

Hence, through the wonderful path of bhakti, the elevation of our mental state is easily achieved. This brings us to the fifth divine law:

## The Law of Sublimation

*The sovereign recipe for purifying the mind and its thoughts is to dovetail it towards the Supreme through bhakti.*

Attachment to the Supreme does not spoil the mind, on the contrary, it purifies the mind. God is all-pure, so when the mind is attached to Him, it also gets cleaned. In fact, the saints and scriptures go a step further and say that true cleansing of the mind can only happen when we absorb our mind in loving devotion to the Lord.

The Ramayan states:

*prema bhagati jala binu raghurāī,*
*abhi antara mala kabahuñ na jāī*

'Until we wash our mind in the water of love for Lord Ram, the dirt within will not go.'

And Jagadguru Shankaracharya wrote:

*śhuddhayati hi nāntarātmā kṛiṣhṇapadāmbhoja bhaktimṛite*
*vasanamiva kśhārodairbhaktyā prakṣhālyate chetaḥ*
(*Prabodh Sudhākar* 167)

'The mind and intellect will not get cleansed without devotion to the lotus feet of Lord Krishna. Just as a garment gets cleansed with soap and water.'

In bhakti, all the infirmities of the mind get sublimated and purified. So, let me give you some examples of how desire, greed, anger, and pride can be channelled in devotion.

***The desires become:***

- 'I am eager to cleanse my heart.'
- 'I wish to please God with my every action.'
- 'I yearn to see the Divine.'

***The greed becomes:***

- 'I want to serve my Lord even more.'
- 'I yearn to develop even more detachment.'
- 'I hanker to enhance my knowledge to understand my Lord better.'

***The anger becomes:***

- 'I am fed up with my stupid mind, which refuses to stay at the lotus feet of my Supreme Beloved. I must work on it even harder.'
- 'Why am I not able to overcome my worldly attachments? I must strive more vigorously in my effort for self-improvement.'

***The pride becomes:***

- 'My Beloved Lord is so wonderful. I am proud of Him.'
- 'I am most fortunate to have the opportunity to express my devotion to Him.'

Do carefully note the thoughts and emotions expressed above in loving devotion. They express yearning for service, sacrifice, and devotion to the Supreme. Who can say that desire, greed, anger, and attachment are bad? These are simple examples of sublime and devotional emotions.

Therefore, **by dovetailing our mind to God, we can develop the richest and noblest sentiments that we humans are capable**

**of.** Those very sentiments, which were previously our worst enemies sitting within, are now transformed into our best friends. And we are well on our way to awakening our best self.

The *Narad Bhakti Darshan* guides us to do the same:

*tadarpitākhilāchāraḥ san kāmakrodhābhimānādikaṁ*
*tasminneva karaṇīyam* (Sutra 65)

'Offer all actions and emotions to the Lord. Even desire, anger, and pride should be directed towards Him.' Then, they all serve to uplift us.

Bhakti means immense love for the Lord. In it, we develop an intense longing to see Him, to meet Him, and to be with Him. Whatever we do, the mind remains attached to God and thoughts flow towards Him like rivers to the ocean. Such love in the heart cleans it of all impurities. With a pure heart, we start seeing the divinity in all living beings and in all things. That is the glory of devotion.

In the remaining sections of this chapter, we will discuss how to dovetail our mind towards God in bhakti. As usual, we will progress logically and sequentially, one step at a time.

## Existence of God

Before we get into devotion, we must first address the question: Is there a God? This question has been asked innumerable times in the past, is being asked in the present, and will continue to be asked in future. Various saints and scriptures have addressed this query in various ways.

We begin with the *Vedānt Darshan*, which states: *janmādyasya yataḥ* (1.1.2) 'The Supreme Divine Entity is He from Whom the entire universe has manifested.' The universe in which we live is so vast and complex, that an all-knowing, all-powerful Creator must be behind it.

Jagadguru Shankaracharya uses the same logic to establish the existence of Brahman:

*yadidaṁ jagaddeva-gandharva-yakṣha-rakṣhaḥ*
*pitṛipiśhāchādi lakṣhaṇaṁ dyuvi yatpṛithivyādityachandrag*
*rahanakṣhatravichitraṁ,*
*vividhaprāṇyupabhoga yogyasādhana sambandhitadatyanta*
*kuśhalaśhilpibhirapi durnirmāṇaṁ* (*Shāṅkar Bhāṣhya*)

He states that this universe, inhabited by celestial gods, *gandharvas*, *yakshas*, demons, and other souls with countless suns, stars, planets, and moons, cannot have been created by a human. There must be a Supreme Creator behind it.

The *Nyaya Darshan* explains God in different manner:

*īśhvaraḥ kāraṇaṁ puruṣha karmāphalya darśhanāt* (4.1.19)

It states that the Law of Karma is visible in the world. One businessperson works hard all his life but fails to succeed. Another puts in extraordinarily little effort and gets huge success. This makes us believe a Law of Karma must be responsible for this inequality. However, karma is insentient by itself; it cannot fructify into results. There is need for an all-powerful personality who notes the karmas, keeps account of them, and bestows their fruits at the proper time. That all-powerful and all-knowing personality is God.

The *Bṛihadāraṇyak Upaniṣhad* presents a third argument:

*etasya vā akṣharasya praśhāsane gārgidvāyā pṛithivyau*
*vidhṛite tiṣhṭhataḥ* (3.8.9)

The verses states that just as a twig held by a bird in its beak drops to the ground as soon as the bird lets go of it, in the same way, this creation which includes innumerable universes cannot be upheld without an Almighty Upholder.

The bottom line is that belief in God requires faith. Existence of God cannot be proven with 100 per cent accuracy and facts. For the purpose of our discussion here, these arguments will suffice. We will now move ahead in our discussion regarding how to develop bhakti.

## Nature of God

The Upanishads are a section of the Vedas that present profound philosophical dissertations. They are respected worldwide for being amongst the highest texts of philosophy in the history of humankind. In the nineteenth century, when he first read them, Arthur Schopenhauer, the German philosopher, put them on his head and began dancing. He wrote: 'There is nothing in this world as elevating as the Upanishads. They have been the solace of my life and they shall be the solace of my death.'

Subsequently, Professor Max Müller declared: 'If these words of Schopenhauer require any confirmation, I shall gladly give it as the result of my lifelong study of the Vedic scriptures.'

Paul Deussen, another famous philosopher, remarked: 'Eternal philosophical truth has seldom found a more striking and decisive expression than in the emancipating knowledge of the philosophy of the Upanishads.'

We see that these Upanishads are so highly revered even by western thinkers. But the principles they propound are very esoteric. Some people say the reason Indians excel in IT skills—

related to virtual cyber space—is because for thousands of years they have been habituated to dealing with the intangible concepts of the Upanishads.

I mention this here because, in this section, we will delve into Vedic and Upanishadic concepts on the nature of God. It is possible you may find the discussion too abstruse or even overwhelming. In that case, you can simply skip forward to the next section, 'Developing Love for God'. But please do not conclude that the whole book is equally complicated. So here goes ...

The *Brahma Purāṇ* informs us:

*asthūlo naṇurūposā vaviśhvo viśhva eva cha*
*viruddha dharmarūpo sā vaiśhvaryāt puruṣhottamaḥ*

**'The Supreme Divine Entity possesses innumerable contradictory attributes at the same time.'** What are some of these mutually opposite qualities? The *Śhwetāśhvatar Upaniṣhad* states:

*aṇoraṇīyān mahato mahīyā-nātmā guhāyāṁ nihito 'sya jantoḥ* (3.20)

This Vedic mantra states that He is subtler than the subtlest—He is present even in the tiniest atomic particle. Yet, He is also bigger than the biggest—all of creation is seated within Him.

These are mutually contradictory qualities of the Supreme Divine Personality. But the Vedas do not stop here. They go on to say that He is beyond all attributes:

*neti natyasthūlamananaṇuḥ* (Vedas)

'No descriptives can circumscribe the Infinite. He is neither "big" nor "small"'. This Vedic mantra is a direct opposite of the previous mantra, yet both are correct. Such is the paradoxical nature of God.

Now, let us see what the *Kaṭhopaniṣhad* states:

*anyatra dharmādanyatrādharmādanyatrāsmāt kṛitākṛitāt*
*anyatra bhūtāchcha bhavyāchcha yat tatpaśhyasi tad vada*
(1.2.14)

'The Supreme is above dharma and adharma; He is beyond cause and effect. He is not limited to past, present, or future. He is also beyond the reach of all empirical experience.' Further, the *Puruṣha Sūktam* states:

*ajāyamāno bahudhā vijāyate tasya yoniṃ paripaśyanti dhīrāḥ*

'He is unborn, and yet He takes innumerable births. The wise know Him as the origin of the universe.'

He is not limited to one form either. The *Ṛig Veda* states:

*ekaṁ sadviprāḥ bahudhā vadanti* (1-164.46)

'Though the Absolute Truth is one, scholars worship Him in various forms.'

Is God male or female? The *Śhwetāśhvatar Upaniṣhad* states that He is both:

*tvaṁ strī tvaṁ pumānasi tvaṁ kumāra uta vā kumārī* (4.3)

'Thou art a Woman, Thou art a Man; Thou art a Youth and a Maiden too. Thou even manifesteth as an old person, tottering with a staff.'

Hence, Narayan and Lakshmi, these are both forms of the Supreme, and so are Krishna and Radha, Ram and Sita, and Shiv and Parvati.

I would like to mention here, that language has its limitations. Thus, in absence of universally accepted phraseology, I refer to God as 'He'. But **from the Vedic perspective, God is both 'He' and 'She'.**

Above are just a few of the innumerable divine attributes of the Lord to help you appreciate His immanence. But the important question is: how do we cultivate bhakti towards Him?

## Developing Love for God

In the previous section, we discussed the almightiness of God. This knowledge engenders reverence for Him but not intimate loving devotion. Sometimes people talk about being God-fearing, but there is a big difference between fearing God and loving Him.

That was what Arjun realized during the Bhagavad Gita. First, he asked Lord Krishna to reveal His universal form. But on seeing it, Arjun became petrified. He states in the Bhagavad Gita:

*danṣhṭrā-karālāni cha te mukhāni*
*dṛiṣhṭvaiva kālānala-sannibhāni*
*diśho na jāne na labhe cha śharma*
*prasīda deveśha jagan-nivāsa* (11.25)

Arjun was so terrified on seeing the cosmic form of the Lord that his mouth dried up and skin felt scorched. He lost his previous loving emotions and developed dread for God. Hence, he requested the Lord to hide the universal form, and once again reveal His loving two-armed form.

We see from this instance that fearing God is a crude and primal form of bhakti. How can we go beyond it and develop actual devotion?

This is a vitally important question, and I am going to give you a simple answer in just two sentences. The details will follow thereafter. **We will develop love for God by establishing our loving relationship with Him. To do this, we must repeatedly think, 'He is mine and I am His.'**

Let me illustrate it through some mundane examples.

*A hundred years ago, Indian society was still highly conservative. Very often, before marriage, the boy and girl would not even see each other. Their parents would decide the marriage. Now, visualize what would happen at such a wedding.*

*The girl has a veil over her face. On panditji's request, the bridegroom and bride recite the mantras. They tie the knot and take the seven circles around the fire. The ceremony is complete, and they are sitting side-by-side before the fire.*

*They have not yet seen each other. But love has already developed. The girl thinks, 'This man sitting on my right is so nice, I love him. He is my husband.'*

*Enquire from the bride, 'Have you seen your husband as yet?'*

*She responds, 'No, I have not. I am still wearing the veil.'*

*'Then how did you develop love for him?'*

*'Because he is mine. I will spend all my life with him. He will love me and take care of me.'*

This is how human psychology works. The moment our intellect decides 'This person is mine', the mind develops love. Similarly, when we decide that our eternal relationship is with God, we will experience loving sentiments for Him.

Let me give you another example, again from a hundred years ago.

*Two girls are walking down a road. A boy is following them. He is passing irreverential comments within their earshot. One of the girls loses her temper. She lifts a slipper in her hand and turns around, 'Let this rogue come close. Today, I will teach him a lesson.'*

*However, her friend scolds her. 'What are you doing? Don't you know he is the boy with whom your parents have arranged your engagement?'*

*Hearing that, the girl's anger subsides. She drops her slipper and looks back with love in her eyes. 'Is he still coming? I hope he has not gone away.'*

What changed suddenly for the girl? How did anger transform into affection? It was the thought, 'This boy is mine. He is my future husband. My self-interest will be fulfilled from him.'

In both these examples, the decision of the intellect 'He is mine' resulted in loving affection. The same formula applies to God as well. When we decide 'The Supreme Lord is mine and I Am His', we will develop love for Him.

## Our Eternal Relationship with God

In the case of the bride and bridegroom, they were creating an association between two human beings through the ceremony of the wedding. However, with God there is no need for such a ritual. As His little fragments, we are eternally a part of Him. He is so close to us that there is not a hair's breadth of gap between Him and us. The Lord is seated within us, and we are seated within Him. The Shreemad Bhagavatam states:

*kṛiṣhṇam enam avehi tvam ātmānam akhilātmanām*

(10.14.55)

'Know Lord Krishna to be the Soul of all the souls in all creation. Just as we are the soul and we have a body, similarly, all the souls in creation are the body of God, and He is the Soul of their souls.' That is proximity of God. It has two specialties.

1. ***God is our eternal relative.***

In endless past lives, in whichever species we received birth, He accompanied us as the *Paramātmā* in the heart. Worldly relatives kept changing—in every life, we had a different father, mother, sister, brother, and friends. However, God remained our eternal Father, Mother, Friend, and Relative.

2. ***God is our selfless relative.***

In the world, people love us for the sake of their own happiness. Their affection is tinged with selfishness. Hence, it fluctuates based on the fulfilment of self-interest. But God does not need anything from us. He loves us selflessly and desires only our welfare.

**Therefore, our eternal and selfless relative is the Supreme Lord. With Him alone is our deepest and closest relationship.** The problem is that since innumerable lifetimes, we have forgotten our connection with Him. To remember it will require effort—we will need to do sadhana.

Consider the following example.

*Ramesh and Dinesh had been buddies in college. But their careers took them to different places. Twenty-five years later, Ramesh was walking in Connaught Place, in Delhi, and he recognized Dinesh walking ahead.*

*Ramesh went and thumped him on his back. 'What a pleasant surprise, Dinesh! I can't believe my eyes it is you.'*

*Dinesh did not recollect his friend. 'Excuse me, but do we know each other?'*

*'You did not recognize me? I was your classmate in Kirori Mal College.'*

*'Hmmm ... I faintly remember it,' responded Dinesh hazily. 'Tell me more.'*

*'We would often sit together at the campus canteen,' Ramesh further reminded.*

*'Yes, it is coming back to me now.'*

*'We were both in our college cricket team,' Ramesh helped with further information.*

*'Oh ... I remember now. You are Ramesh! Wow, this is so wonderful. What a delight to meet you after a quarter of a century!'*

We see how Dinesh and Ramesh were friends, but Dinesh had forgotten, so effort was needed to recall. Similarly, our connection with God is eternal, but we do not remember. Therefore, **some effort will be required to recollect our bond with Him. That effort is called 'Sadhana Bhakti', or preparatory devotion.** Let us understand the way to practise it.

## The Five Sentiments of Bhakti

*In ancient times, there would be the ruler of a country. Everyone connected with him differently. The common citizens saw him as their king. Their relationship with him was a far and distant one.*

*The same king had his retinue of servants. They saw him as their master, and they would even receive direct instructions from him. The king was the same, but the relationship had grown closer.*

*The king also had his personal friends. They had grown up with him, playing games together in childhood. They still looked on the king as their buddy.*

*Then there were the king's children, who used to sit in his lap when they were little. For them, he was their father first, and the regent of the land later.*

*Finally, there was the queen. She related to the king most intimately and was familiar with all his personal idiosyncrasies. She often addressed him as 'Darling'. The king was the same person, but the relationship had become even dearer.*

In this example, everyone related to the one king in different ways. Similarly, there are five bhavs (sentiments) in devotion towards the One Almighty Lord. These are five ways for taking our mind to Him. They have been detailed in the various bhakti scriptures, such as the *Narad Bhakti Darshan*, the *Bhakti Rasāmṛit Sindhu, Prem Ras Siddhānt*, and so on.

The five bhavs of bhakti are:

### 1. ***Śhānt bhav*** **(devotion in the passive sentiment)**

In it, we think, 'The Lord is my King.' For example, the residents of Dwarika looked upon Lord Krishna as their Ruler. The residents of Ayodhya saw Lord Ram as their Sovereign. This sentiment is quite common in Christianity too, where God is seen as the King of heaven.

However, feelings towards a king are of awe and reverence. 'When the king's procession comes to my side of the town, I will go and see him from afar, and exclaim, "Look, there goes our King!"' But can we also go and sit at His Majesty's feet, chat with him, and offer personal service? No, citizens do not have these privileges; they can only revere the king from a distance.

In *śhānt* bhav, feelings of respect and admiration dominate; the idea of our personal intimate connection with God does not get nurtured. The higher bhavs offer sweeter and more intimate ways to connect with Him.

2. ***Dāsya bhav*** **(sentiment of servitude)**

Here, we see ourselves as the servants of the Lord. This sentiment is again quite common. In this bhav, the Lord is now our Master and we are His servants. In many religious traditions around the world, devotees connect with God in the attitude of servitude.

*Dāsya* bhav also includes the fraternal and maternal sentiments, i.e., looking upon the Lord as our Father or Mother. The most popular example of this bhav is Hanuman—he looks upon himself as the servitor of Lord Ram.

3. ***Sakhya bhav*** **(fraternal sentiment of devotion)**

In this bhav, in immense love towards the Lord, the sense of awe and reverence gets neglected. Instead, we now see Him as our dearest friend. The Vedas state: *dvā suparṇā sayujā sakhāyā* (*Muṇḍaka Upaniṣhad* 3.1.1) 'Like two birds on a branch, the soul and its friend, the Supreme Soul, both reside within the body.'

An example of a devotee in *sakhya* bhav was Arjun, who considered Lord Krishna as a dear comrade. That is why he did not hesitate to have the Lord drive his chariot during the Mahabharat. In the *Ram-leela*, Sugreev related to Lord Ram as his friend.

In Shree Krishna's Vrindavan pastimes, the devotion of the *gwāl-bālas*, cowherd boys, was in *sakhya* bhav. Their interactions with Him were so intimate that even Brahma became confused on seeing them. He states in the Bhagavatam:

*aho bhāgyam aho bhāgyaṁ nanda-gopa-vrajaukasām*
*yan-mitraṁ paramānandaṁ pūrṇaṁ brahma sanātanam*
(10.14.32)

'How greatly fortunate are these cowherd boys in Nanda baba's land of Braj! The Supreme Divine Lord, who is always the ocean of divine bliss, has become their intimate friend.'

### 4. ***Vātsalya bhav*** **(maternal or paternal sentiment)**

To understand this sentiment, let us first consider a mundane example.

*Suppose there is a police commissioner of a certain city. Hundreds salute him and thousands fear him. But his mother only sees the police commissioner as her son. She does not care for his designation. In fact, she even scolds him, 'My child, why are you neglecting your health nowadays?'*

Similarly, in *vātsalya* bhav, the devotee feels, 'The Lord is my child. I must take care of Him.' This is the bhav of Dashrath and Kaushalya towards Lord Ram. It is also the sentiment of Nanda baba and Mother Yashoda towards Shree Krishna.

### 5. ***Mādhurya bhav*** **(conjugal sentiment)**

In this bhav, we feel so closely related to the Lord, that we look upon Him as our Beloved. This is how the *gopīs* of Vrindavan worshipped Shree Krishna. In South India, the love of Andal for Lord Ranganath is a famous example of *mādhurya* bhav. Another famous example of the conjugal sentiment in devotion is Meera Bai. She looked upon the Lord as her beloved, and in this way, felt deeply connected with Him.

**The five bhavs are five pathways for taking our mind to God.** Another word for bhakti is *upāsanā*. *Asana* means 'to sit' and *up* is 'close to'. Hence, *upāsanā* implies 'to sit close to God', or literally, to take the mind close to God. The five sentiments we have discussed help us in our devotion as we shall see in the next section.

## Advantages of the Five Sentiments of Bhakti

The Vedic philosophy is not limited to one lifetime. We have all had infinite lives, and in every lifetime, we had relatives—father, mother, sister, brother, son, daughter, husband, wife, aunts, uncles, and so on. Hence, we have *sanskārs* (tendencies) for desiring all kinds of love. We desire a mother's and also a father's love; we want a friend's love and also the spouse's love.

Let us say, a man has a wife, sister, and daughter, but his mother died during his birth. He missed receiving maternal care. When he sees his friends being pampered by their mothers, he laments, 'If only I had a mother. Then I too would have received this kind of affection.'

We want all kinds of love. These are our *sanskārs*. The path of bhakti teaches us to dovetail all these sentiments towards the Lord.

Hence, Lord Krishna instructed us to look upon God as our Everything.

*tam eva śharaṇaṁ gachchha sarva-bhāvena bhārata*
(Bhagavad Gita 18.62)

'O Arjun, with every bhav surrender to the Lord. See Him as your All.'

Echoing this sentiment, Gandhari said to Lord Krishna:

*tvameva mātā cha pitā tvameva,*
*tvameva bandhuśhcha sakhā tvameva*

*tvameva vidyā draviṇam tvameva,*
*tvameva sarvaṁ mama deva deva* (*Pāṇḍav Gītā*)

'You are truly my Mother and Father. You alone are my Relative and Friend. You are truly my Knowledge and Wealth. You truly are my All, my God of gods.'

Depending upon which form of the Supreme we wish to worship, we can adopt some or all these five bhavs. Not all these bhavs can be practiced towards every form of the Lord. Undoubtedly, we can keep all these bhavs towards Lord Krishna as revealed in His divine pastimes of Vrindavan.

The *Bhakti Rasāmṛit Sindhu* states:

*yena kena prakāreṇa manaḥ kṛiṣhṇe niveśhayeta*

'By whatever means possible, take your mind to the Lord.'

Each of these five sentiments described above is a powerful way to sublimate our emotional tendencies towards God.

## Benefits of Attaching the Mind to God

Having discussed how to sublimate our mind towards God, I will mention just a few of its innumerable benefits.

***The first benefit*** is that by absorbing the mind in the all-pure Lord, the mind gets purified as well.

***The second benefit*** is that our lower nature—desire, anger, greed, and pride—get sublimated in devotion. They all become noble and sentiments that work to our advantage.

We have already discussed both these points in detail earlier in the chapter so, let us move on.

***The third benefit*** is that when we have love for God, we automatically start doing everything for His pleasure. This results in karm yog.

Karm yog basically means 'karm' plus 'bhakti'. It is the predominant instruction of the Bhagavad Gita: *tasmāt sarveṣhu kāleṣhu mām anusmara yudhya cha* (8.7) 'Do your work with your body, and keep the mind absorbed in God.'

Hence, **in karm yog, the intention behind every work gets purified. 'How can my actions be pleasing to the Lord?' That purity of intention makes the most significant difference to our life.**

*Take the example of Arjun. He was a warrior before hearing the Bhagavad Gita. After hearing the divine scripture, he was still a warrior. What transformed was his intention. Earlier his motive was to gain control over a kingdom. Later, he was simply doing a duty that had befallen upon him as a service to the Lord. The change was not in his actions but in his intention. This was an example of karm yog. Arjun's mind was in God, while he performed his worldly duties physically.*

The understanding of the principle of karm yog empowers us to grow from within to become a better person. Sometimes people have the mistaken notion that engaging in bhakti somehow means to become less effective in our worldly works. But that is an incorrect understanding. You continue to perform your worldly duties, but the intention becomes divine.

Let us say you are a businessman. Without bhakti, the intention would be selfish: 'Let me earn money so that I can enjoy in the world.' Now, when bhakti develops in the heart, you still do business, but the intention becomes divine: 'I will earn lots of money, so that after taking care of my daily necessities, I can serve God with it.'

Now, when our intention is to please God with our works, we do them even better than before. There is an interesting story illustrating this concept.

*Akbar was a famous Mughal king during the medieval period of Indian history. In his council of ministers was a great musician, called Tansen. He was said to be so proficient in music that with* Rāga Megh Mālhar, *he could make rain fall, and with* Rāga Dīpak, *make lamps light up.*

*One day, Akbar asked him, 'Tansen! You sing so well. Who is the guru who taught you such music?'*

*Tansen replied, 'O King! My guru is Swami Haridas. He resides in Vrindavan, the holy land of Shree Krishna.'*

*Tansen then proceeded to take Akbar to Vrindavan to meet his guru. There, Akbar got the opportunity to hear Swami Haridas sing the sweetest devotional bhajans, and he was thrilled by the heavenly melody.*

*Later, while returning, Akbar asked Tansen, 'Why is it that you cannot sing as well as your guru?'*

*Earlier his question was that when Tansen sang so well, who could his guru be? But now he was reversing his question and asking why Tansen could not match his guru's musical skills.*

*Tansen replied perspicaciously, 'O King! The reason should have been obvious to you. I sing for the pleasure of the king of Hindustan. My guru sings for the pleasure of the King of the world. The source of inspiration that guruji has within himself can never be matched by me.'*

The story highlights the power of pure intention. Tansen's guru was singing in devotion. But that did not mean he was lackadaisical about it. Rather, he was inspired to sing his devotional best. Tansen admitted that his singing was inferior because it did not have purity of intention that comes from bhakti.

***The fourth benefit*** is that since the results of our efforts are for the pleasure of the Supreme, we are not attached to them. If, after our best exertions, the results do not come, we think, 'Probably it was not the will of the Lord. Let me submit to His wish and be happy.' **This sense of detachment from results frees us from stress, anxiety, tension, and fear.**

***The fifth benefit*** of attaching the mind to God is that our self-identity gets transformed. We see ourselves as fragments of the divine. Such an attitude allows us to develop a healthy self-identity based on the reality of our soul instead of one based on ego or people's ideas or perceptions of us. We become humble without being self-demeaning.

***The sixth benefit*** is that our perspective towards others changes. We see everyone with whom we interact as divine (fragments of God) and as a result, we maintain a healthy attitude towards them. Our interpersonal interactions are positive and service oriented.

***The seventh benefit*** is that when we keep God in our consciousness, we realize that His grace makes all things possible. In this manner, we get freedom from the pride of doership.

***The eighth benefit*** of attaching our mind to God is that the goal of human life is God-realization. When we become karm yogis, we move towards the supreme goal of life, together with doing our worldly duties.

In this chapter, we have discussed the techniques for sublimating the mind's thoughts and emotions towards the Supreme. But this will not suffice without knowing the difference between selfish and selfless love. This begs the question: what is true love and how is it different from selfish love? Let us discuss this in the next chapter.

## Key Takeaways

- The level of our consciousness is tied to our mind. Hence, we are only as good as our mind is.
- Attachment, desire, anger, greed, envy, and pride—these create an unholy nexus of thoughts that contaminate our mind. This forms our lower nature.
- But we also have a higher nature that dislikes the lower impulses and struggles to give them up.
- The problem is that suppression has the reverse effect—the thoughts we suppress become more persistent.
- In bhakti, we do not stop the thinking process; instead, we dovetail the mind towards God. This makes our desires and attachments divine.
- To develop bhakti, we must establish our loving relationship with the Lord, by repeatedly thinking, 'He is mine and I am His.'
- The five bhavs of devotion are five pathways for taking our mind to the Lord.
- The practice of karm yog entails that we do all our works with our mind absorbed in Him.

# 6

# The Law of Love

Relationships are among the most important aspects of human life. Aristotle, the legendary Greek philosopher, wrote: 'Man is by nature a social animal. Society is something that precedes the individual.'

Ultimately, our eternal relative is God. Yet, as long as we live in this world, we cannot avoid human interactions and social links. Some relationships we choose like those with friends; others we inherit like those with parents and siblings; and some networks we are thrust into like those with classmates and office colleagues.

For a happy and successful life, we are required to adroitly navigate all these relationships with positivity and maturity. There are many benefits of successfully nurturing relationships:

- Networks help us get social support. We develop a sense of being part of something bigger than ourselves.

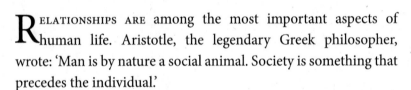

- Relationships help us cultivate the spirit of caring for others. We develop the virtues of compassion and sacrifice.
- Proper connections enable us to receive help from others in our personal growth. We find support and mentorship in our work environment.
- Healthy relationships enhance our health. We get an outlet for unwinding, relaxing, and reducing stress. Scientific studies reveal that emotional support is a great health enhancer. Julianne Holt-Lunstad, one of the first researchers to correlate the link between social support and death, noted, 'A lack of social relationships was equivalent to smoking up to 15 cigarettes a day.'
- Supportive relationships increase the longevity of our life. Studies conducted on centenarians reveal the secret of their longevity lies in the emotional support they receive from family, friends, and relatives.

These are only a few of the innumerable benefits of healthy and dependable connections. At the same time, the biggest cause of anxiety, disharmony, and dissatisfaction in life is also relationships. Any spiritual or psychological counsellor will tell you from personal experience that about half the times people come to them with relational problems. That means fifty per cent of the problems we face in life are due to interpersonal dealings. Thus, **relationships are like a double-edged sword and it is important to learn how to handle them effectively.**

Establishing meaningful and trustworthy relationships is easy for some. They nurture positive connections and reap the benefits in terms of personal fulfilment and professional success. But most people make an utter mess of their relationships. Later, when they experience interpersonal grief, they blame luck and destiny for it. Consequently, understanding what makes relationships work is essential to be happy and effective in life.

## Expectations Ruin Relationships

Sometimes relational friction is unavoidable but at other times we bring it upon ourselves by our own faulty attitudes. Consider the following example.

*One three-year-old boy is walking beside his mother in a supermarket. With his little hand, he is holding the frills of his mother's dress. There is profuse sweetness in his gestures, as he castes glances with a beaming smile on his face. He looks like a little angel.*

*However, at the checkout counter, a change happens. He looks at the milk chocolate jar and points it to his mother, 'Mommy, I want a chocolate.'*

*Now, if his mother fulfils his desire, then his sweetness continues as before. But if by chance, his mother refuses, then all hell breaks loose. He screams and sobs uncontrollably, tugging at his mother's clothes, and stomping his little feet on the floor. His tantrum is so intense that it makes his mother repent, 'Why did I ever have a child, if I had to see this day?'*

If you happened to have witnessed this scene, you would have wondered what transformed the boy so dramatically? One moment he was an angel, and the next moment, he turned into a little imp.

It was a case of unfulfilled expectations. So long as his wishes were getting satisfied, everything was all right. But the moment his mother did not care to give him what he wanted, he was enraged.

This is precisely the case with us as well. In human relationships, we behave very much like that little boy. **We want others to act in certain ways, and when they do not, we feel we have the right to become upset. In this way, unfulfilled expectations strain relationships.**

This principle applies to all kinds of relationships—husband-wife, siblings, friends, boss-subordinate, child-parent, etc. Here are some common examples of expectations in our interactions:

- I want that others should behave in ways that make me happy.
- I want that others' mood should match my mood.
- I want that others should understand me.
- I want that others' perspective should match mine.
- I want that others should not make mistakes.

Each of these are self-centred desires. They are based upon the attitude, 'What's in it for me?' But the irony is that we dupe ourselves into believing they are for the other's sake. We even declare that we are offering selfless service, yet the selfishness remains hidden within. This is like putting a garb of holiness on top of our unholiness.

**If our expectations were genuinely selfless, their unfulfillment would not have upset us.** But the fact that we get annoyed means we are selfish; we expect our own happiness from others.

*One gentleman came and said to me, 'Swamiji, I am going to leave the temple community.'*

*I asked him, 'Pray tell me the reason for your annoyance.'*

*He responded, 'I served the temple so selflessly, but nobody gave me the due recognition for it.'*

*I thought to myself, 'If you were so selfless, then you would not have required any recognition. Your annoyance is because of selfish expectations though you may not realize it.'*

Our selfishness exists even in our interactions with the Supreme. Often, people say they have lost faith in God. I ask them the reason for it. They say, 'We entreated Him for something, and He did not fulfil our wishes. So now we have lost faith.'

These people expected something from God. When that did not happen, they became upset. They stopped their devotion, without even pausing to think, 'Maybe my own desires were unholy.' After all, **God is not a waiter in a restaurant that every time we press the bell, He should appear to receive our order, 'Yes sir, what can I do for you?'**

The problem here is not with God but with our own self-seeking attitude. Like the three-year-old boy in the supermarket, we get upset whenever our wishes are thwarted. We grow up physically but remain childish emotionally.

Now listen to the most astonishing fact. Everyone in this material world is selfish to varying degrees. The Vedas state:

*na vā are sarvasya kāmāya sarvaṁ priyaṁ bhavaty ātmanas*
*tu kāmāya sarvaṁ priyaṁ bhavati ātmā vā are draṣhṭavyaḥ*
*śhrotavyo mantavyo nididhyāsitavyo maitreyi*

(*Bṛihadāraṇyak Upaniṣhad* 2.4.5)

In this Vedic mantra, Sage Yagyavalkya explains to his wife Maitreyi that everybody loves others, not for the others' sake, but for their own sake. Understanding the reality of worldly relationships, one should reflect, contemplate, and meditate upon God.

The Shreemad Bhagavatam states:

*sarveṣhām api bhūtānāṁ nṛipa svātmaiva vallabhaḥ*
*itare 'patya-vittādyās tad-vallabhatayaiva hi* (10.14.50)

'All living beings consider themselves as most dear. Others—children, wealth, and so on—are dear only for the sake of the self.'

The Ramayan states:

*sura nara muni saba kī yaha rītī,*
*svāratha lāgi karahiṅ saba prītī*

'Celestial gods, humans, and pandits—all have the same nature. Wherever their self-interest is met, they develop affection.'

What is the cause for our intrinsic unholy selfishness? The reason for it is that we souls are all tiny parts of God, who is an ocean of infinite happiness. Since every part is attracted towards its source, we are naturally drawn to bliss. Thus, everything we do is for the sake of our own happiness. And we look to others to make or keep us happy as well.

We will rise above selfishness when we learn and practice the secret of divine love. Let's understand the secret.

## Love, Lust, and Business

Love is one of the strongest forces of human nature. We all seek to receive love from others. We also wish to offer our love to others. But if the question were asked, 'Do you know what love is?', very few people would be able to give a satisfactory answer.

To understand love, let us compare three things: 1) love, 2) lust, and 3) business. The opposite of love is lust, and business lies between them.

- **Love *(prem)*:** Where we seek to give, give, give, that is love. **When our goal in a relationship is to serve and give happiness to the other, it is true love.** It is an exceedingly rare and sublime thing. We can also refer to it as divine love.
- **Lust *(kām)*:** When we want to take, take, take, that is lust. We usually look on lust as sensual desire. But the Vedic scriptures give a broader definition: The self-seeking nature (or selfish intention) in a relationship is lust.
- **Business *(vyāpār)*:** If we engage in reciprocity i.e., give-and-take, give-and-take, that is business. Such a relationship is like barter.

With knowledge of the distinction between the three, we now come to the sixth divine law:

## The Law of Love

*Our hearts can only be satisfied by true love, which is a deep and noble affection for the others' happiness, without seeking personal benefit in return.*

In endless past lives, we practised *kām* and *vyāpār* but never *prem*. Even if we give, it is always with an eye for getting something in return.

One man is invited to his friend's daughter's wedding. He ponders what gift he should give to them. He decides on giving them one lakh rupees. Now, you ask him, why is he being so generous? Has he become '*dānī* Karna' (like the famous charity-giver Karna)? He will respond that he has three daughters, and they will soon get married. So, his friend will be obliged to match the gift and give one lakh each time!

You see, that is the formula we all have. We first think, 'What's in it for me?' and then we give to the other. Thus, our relationships are transactional like that of a shopkeeper.

*A shopkeeper owns a watch shop in Kalbadevi market in Mumbai. In the morning, he cleans his shop, arranges his watches on the display panels, and lights incense before the altar. Now he stands outside waiting for customers.*

*Let us say, you are passing by his shop. He beckons, 'Come ... come ... come.'*

*Seeing such polite behaviour, you think he must be a very nice man. You ask him, 'Tell me, where is the chappal (shoe) shop in Kalbadevi?'*

*'Chappal shop?' the shopkeeper responds, visibly annoyed. 'Can you not see this is a watch shop?'*

*'That is right,' you say. 'But I want chappals. It is my first visit to Kalbadevi. Please guide me to the nearest shoe shop.'*

*'I do not have time,' says the shopkeeper. 'Move ahead.' Two minutes earlier, he seemed to have such love for you, but it suddenly disappeared.*

*If you wish to evoke his love for you again, it will not be difficult. Simply ask him, 'Watches? Oh, I needed a wristwatch as well. Do you have the HMT brand?'*

*'Yes, of course! Come ... come ... come.' Again, he loves you so much!*

*You walk into his shop, and he begins showing you piece after piece, until there are twenty watches on the display board. 'Do not take out so many,' you say to him. 'I only want one.'*

*He responds politely, 'I am your servant, Madam! If you do not like them, I will put them back.'*

*What kind of servant he is gets revealed when the price is discussed. The bargaining goes back and forth, but then he realizes he cannot make any profit from you. Again, he becomes detached, 'If the price doesn't suit you, please leave.' His love has again disappeared.*

See how this shopkeeper's love is swinging up and down, like a roller coaster, based on his self-interest. Unfortunately, the same thing happens in all relationships as well. Five times in a day, we change our decision about others. For instance, a husband thinks: 'My wife is wonderful', 'No, she is merely good', 'Well, actually she is just normal', 'In fact, my wife is bad', 'No, she is awful!'

How come this husband's opinion about his wife is varying so much? It is a simple computation. When he feels that she is fulfilling his self-interest, she is good. When he perceives that she is not giving him happiness but not harming either, then she is normal. And when he thinks she is harming his self-interest, then she is bad.

We have observed how sentiments towards our loved ones keep seesawing. It means what we assume to be love is not genuine love. What, then, is true love in relationships?

## The Test of True Love

Believe it or not, there is a test to identify true love. What is it? True love is that where there is a reason for it to be destroyed, and yet it continues unabated.

Sage Rupa Goswami wrote:

*sarvathā dhvaṁsa rahitaṁ satyapi dhvaṁsa kāraṇe*
*yadbhāva bandhanaṁ yūnoḥ sa premā parikīrtitaḥ*
(*Ujjwal Neelmani* verse 14.63)

**'Where there is ample reason for love to be devastated, and yet it continues unabated, that is true love.'** Let me share with you a deeply touching story of this kind of love as related by a medical attendant.

*One morning, around 9.00 a.m., an elderly gentleman in his 80s came to the minor operation theatre to get his stitches removed from his thumb. He requested me to remove them quickly since he had an appointment at a nearby nursing home at 9.30 a.m.*

*While I was taking his vitals, I asked him if the other appointment was also with a doctor? He said he had to join his wife for breakfast.*

*I asked him about his wife's health. He revealed that as a victim of Alzheimer's, she had been in the nursing home for three months now.*

*I asked him if she would be upset if he got late. He replied that her Alzheimer's was in such a progressive stage now that she had not recognized him in five years.*

*His answer surprised me. I asked him, 'Even though she does not recognize you, yet you go every morning to meet her?'*

*He smiled and patted my shoulder and said, 'Fifty-five years ago, I had made a commitment to her. She does not know who I am, but I do know who she is.'*

How noble was the old man's love for his wife! It was full of acceptance, stability, and sacrifice. This is true love, not the affection of fair-weather friends that comes and goes with the seasons.

What is the basis of such pure love? Continue to read the next section to learn about it.

## The Service Attitude

The foundation of true love is a service attitude—the desire to help the other, to benefit the other, without seeking any reward in return. I quote here the famous words of Saint Francis of Assisi:

*O Divine Master, grant that I may not so much seek*
*To be consoled, as to console*
*To be understood, as to understand*
*To be loved, as to love*
*For it is in giving that we receive*
*It is in pardoning that we are pardoned*
*And it is in dying that we are born to eternal life.*

Human relationships are complex matters requiring sacrifice, adjustment, and understanding for their sustenance. **When we look to serve, we do not get heartbroken on seeing others' weaknesses. Instead, we see it as our duty to help them overcome their frailties.** We also do not care for returns, because for the genuine lover, the opportunity to offer our love is the reward itself.

If the foundation of genuine love is a service attitude, then what is the foundation of the desire to serve? It is a natural consequence of developing our Spiritual Quotient (SQ) or Spiritual Intelligence (SI).

SQ is a very nascent concept in the field of human psychology. Scientists are still debating about what it is. The best analysis I have come across is by Danah Zohar in her book *Spiritual Intelligence: The Ultimate Intelligence.* Taking her analysis as a starting point, I have modified it below.

Spiritual Intelligence has four aspects to it:

1. ***Self-awareness skills.*** This is the wisdom related to aspects of your self—self-identity, self-goals, and self-analysis. It includes:
   - Awareness that you are not the perishable body but the eternal soul.
   - Awareness of your lower nature that pulls you down.
   - Awareness of your higher nature that aspires for growth.
   - Awareness of the purpose of your life.
   - Awareness of your values hierarchy.
2. ***Universal awareness skills.*** This is the wisdom to see the connection between everything in the universe. It includes:
   - Awareness of the interconnectedness of all creation.
   - Empathy for the opinions and views of others.
   - Sympathy for the happiness and distress of others.
   - Awareness of the spiritual laws that govern the universe.
3. ***Self-mastery skills.*** This is the ability to put spiritual knowledge into practice in personal and professional life. It includes:
   - Commitment to pursuing your spiritual growth.
   - Commitment to keeping your higher self in-charge.
   - Living according to your values and purpose.
4. ***Social and professional mastery skills.*** This is our ability to make a positive difference in the lives of others. It includes:
   - Serving through your professional work.

- Serving in your personal relationships.
- Serving through your position of leadership.

The modern-day multiple intelligence theory states that all of us possess a variety of kinds of intelligence. Let us see the sequential way in which the major faculties of our intellect start to bloom as we go through the stages of life.

The first intelligence that develops after birth is **Physical Intelligence (PQ).** Sitting, standing, walking, running, and all other such physical activities require control over our musculoskeletal system. As the PQ develops, we learn to manoeuvre our physical body.

The next intelligence to develop is when we enter school. We are required to understand, analyse, and reason. This requires **Cognitive Intelligence (IQ).**

Then, when we reach teenage years, life becomes more complex. We now need to understand and manage our own emotional sentiments and those of others around us. This leads to the development of **Emotional Intelligence (EQ).** Those with high EQ know what they are feeling, what their emotions mean, and how these emotions can affect others.

But then as we enter young adulthood, we begin searching for meaning and purpose in life. That leads to the development of **spiritual skills (SQ).** This develops to different extents in different people. If spiritual intelligence begins to blossom, it brings the realization that we are not cut-off from the universe. We are all integral fragments and energies of God, and our dharma (duty) as His little parts is to serve Him.

*Consider the example of the hand. It is a part of the body, and it serves the body in various ways. It holds the spoon and takes the food from the plate to the mouth; takes the cup of water and holds it to the lips; it applies soap and water to the body for bathing, and so on.*

*Now, suppose one day, the hand gets tired of its service, and says, 'I am fed up. Fifty-five years have gone by serving ... serving ... serving. I have had enough. Sever me from the body. Henceforth, I will live on my own.'*

*Do you think the hand will be able to survive on its own? It will become a mere lump of flesh and bone and will wither in no time. The hand's constitutional position was to serve the body, of which it was an integral part. By doing so, its self-interest was automatically met. It was receiving the nutrition and nourishment it needed from the body.*

Similarly, we too are tiny fragments of the Supreme Divine Personality. The Vedas state:

*chinmātraṁ śrī hareranśhaṁ sūkṣhmamakṣharamavyayam*

'The soul is a part of God; it is sentient, subtle, eternal, and immutable.'

Spiritual wisdom teaches us that just like the hand is a part of the body and serves it faithfully, as tiny fragments of the Lord, it is our inherent nature to serve Him. By doing so, we will automatically receive the bliss, love, and knowledge that our soul is hankering for since eternity.

**If we can perfect our service attitude towards God, we will then look to serve in everything we do. Even in all our relational dealing with others, we will behave in a manner that will please our Beloved Lord.** That is the secret to developing a service attitude in relationships.

So, first we must perfect our love for God. Only then, will we desire to serve in all our dealings. Hence, the remaining portion of the chapter is dedicated to the meaning of true devotion to God.

## Stop Doing Business with God

In the name of devotion, most people do business with the Lord. 'O Hanumanji, if you cure my child's health, I will offer you five kg laddus.' 'O Durga Ma, if my daughter's marriage happens, I will donate a fan in your temple.' This kind of sentiment is not bhakti, it is business.

*One man was walking along a beach in a remote place, when he felt extremely thirsty. Before him was the vast ocean, but it could not quench his thirst as its water was salty. This man's eyes fell upon a coconut tree, laden with fruit. Eagerly, he climbed up its trunk to reach the fruit hanging from a hundred feet above. He chopped a few coconuts and threw them down.*

*But when it was time to get down, he became terrified. Glancing at what lay beneath him, he realized it would be fatal if his feet slipped. In mountain climbing as well, going down is often the more difficult part.*

*The man prayed, 'O Sita Ram, when I was a little child, I used to visit your temple with my mother. If you help me reach down safely today, I will feed 100 brahmins.' With that resolve he began descending slowly.*

*When he had descended half-way, he looked down and felt a bit more secure. He announced, 'Sita Ram, I will not feed a hundred brahmins, but I will feed fifty.'*

*As he continued to descend, he kept reducing his offering to twenty, ten, five, two, and one. Finally, when his feet reached the ground, he said, 'Sita Ram, I had resolved to feed one brahmin. Well, I am a brahmin myself. I will feed myself and You be happy.'*

This attitude is not bhakti, this is business. And most people's devotion is no different. 'O Lord Venkatesh, if my business improves, I will give ten per cent to You.' 'O Lord Ayyappa, do my work and I will fast for forty-one days for You.' 'O Ma Vaishno Devi, if You bless me with a child, I will offer You an embroidered shawl.' Most devotees visiting churches, masjids, gurdwaras, and synagogues have the same attitude as well. They go to God for the fulfilment of their material desires.

The problem with this kind of devotion is that the mind does not get purified. Suppose a devotee goes to the temple for forty days daily, with the prayer, 'O Divine Mother, please cure my son.' Please note what is taking place in such devotion. The devotee's mind is not in the Divine Mother; it is absorbed in the child. The Divine Mother is only a means for curing the son. Can we call this devotion to the Divine Mother? Not really; it is devotion of the son, in care of the Divine Mother. 'If She cannot cure my child, then let me go to Hanuman. If even He cannot cure, let me go to Lord Krishna.' That is how such devotees' psychology works.

People often ask me a question as I travel around the world. 'Swamiji, there is so much religious practice in India. God is worshipped in practically every household in some form or the other. Then why is this devotion not leading to eradication of corruption? Why is the character of people not transforming positively?'

What can be the answer to this question? There is only one answer. **What may seem to be devotion to God is, in fact, devotion to the world because we approach God for the fulfilment of our worldly desires.**

The scriptures label this type of bhakti as *sakām* bhakti. If we wish to purify our mind and awaken our best self, we will have to learn *niṣhkām* bhakti, in which we do not ask God for anything. That is the instruction of all the Vedic scriptures, and I quote below a few such verses.

The Shreemad Bhagavatam states:

*lakṣhaṇaṁ bhakti-yogasya nirguṇasya hy udāhṛitam*
*ahaituky avyavahitā yā bhaktiḥ puruṣhottame* (3.29.12)

'Devotion to the Supreme Divine Personality should be untinged by material aspirations; it should flow without any interruption and be without desire for reward.' The *Bhakti Rasāmṛit Sindhu* similarly states:

*anyābhilāṣhitā-śhūnyaṁ jñāna-karmādy-anāvṛitam*
*ānukūlyena kṛiṣhṇānu-śhīlanaṁ bhaktir uttamā* (1.1.11)

'Engage in devotion to the Supreme Lord with positive loving sentiments and without desire for material profit. Such devotion should be free from philosophic speculation and fruitive activities.'

The *Narad Bhakti Darshan* also states:

*guṇarahitaṁ kāmanārahitaṁ pratikṣhaṇa vardhamānam*
*avichchhinnaṁ sūkṣhmataramanubhavarūpam* (Sutra 54)

'This Love is beyond three modes of material nature, above all desires, grows every moment, and remains incessant. It is subtler than the subtlest and is in the form of an experience.' Chaitanya Mahaprabhu expressed with very strongly:

*kāmera tātparya nija-sambhoga kevala*
*kṛiṣhṇa-sukha-tātparya-mātra prema ta' prabala*
*ataeva kāma-preme bahuta antara*
*kāma — andha-tamaḥ, prema — nirmala bhāskara*
(*Chaitanya Charitāmṛit, Ādi Leela*, 4.166 & 171)

'Where the desire is simply for self-happiness, that is lust; where the desire is desire for Lord Krishna's happiness, that is love. **Lust is like darkness while love is pure like the Sun.**'

All the verses above state that devotion should be unselfish i.e., free from seeking material rewards. Let us now look at what such pure bhakti for God looks like.

## Serving God with Devotion

True bhakti is that which is done for the pleasure of God. The goal is to serve, with whatever we have, for His happiness. For this, **we need faith that in giving to God, we will never lose.**

Rabindranath Tagore was awarded the Nobel Prize in Literature in 1913 for his literary work *Gitanjali*. I am relating below from the poem what I loved most in that anthology.

*There was a beggar, who was fed up with his life of deficiency and hardship. One day, while musing about his miserable existence, he saw the chariot of the King of kings in the distance.*

*The beggar was thrilled at his good fortune. He started daydreaming: 'I am seeing the King of kings! This is my lucky day. It is possible His chariot will turn in my direction. Then, maybe the King of kings will come and greet me. Possibly, He will say, "Mendicant, ask what you want." Then I shall say, "I want this … this … this …"' He began preparing a list of items.*

*That day turned out to be in fact providential for him. The chariot of the King of kings turned towards him and moved forward until it reached right in front. The beggar could not believe what was happening. But the matter did not end there. The King of kings descended from His chariot and stood before him.*

*The mendicant thought, 'This is too good to be true. Am I dreaming?' He pinched himself and realized it was not a dream. He then closed his eyes and started revising the list of items to ask from God.*

*Then, he opened his eyes for the propitious moment but was stunned by what he saw. The King of kings had spread his hand and was saying in a most loving and kindhearted voice, 'O Mendicant! Is there anything you can give Me?'*

*The beggar's intellect failed him. In utter confusion, he could think of nothing better. He dipped his hand into his cloth bag and discovered a grain of wheat. He placed it on the palm of the King of kings, who turned around and took it away.*

*The mendicant returned home, feeling cheated at the turn of events. He had reached the ocean of nectar and was still thirsty. He had now lost the one little remaining grain.*

*However, when he reached his poor hut, there was another surprise in store for him. In his cloth bag was a grain of gold. Now the beggar put two and two together. For the one grain of wheat he had given to the King of kings, he had received a grain of gold in return. The King's asking was His way of giving in return.*

*Now he cursed his intellect. 'Oh My God! I missed my chance. If today I had given my all, everything would have turned into gold. By being miserly, I only hurt myself.'*

The lesson from this story is that even if our goal is to receive from God, it is in giving that we receive. There is a Hindi saying: *bina māṅge motī mile, māṅge mile na bhīkha* **'On asking, you get nothing. And without asking, you get priceless gems.'**

Such is the law of God. Therefore, our sentiments should be along the lines of 'Think not what God can do for you; think what you can do for God.' This is the service attitude.

But what service can the tiny soul offer to the Infinite Lord? This is a natural question that arises. Understand the answer through the illustration below.

*A child went up to his father and said, 'Papa, please give me ten rupees.'*

*'What will you do with it, beta?' asked the father.*

*'I need it. Please ... please ... please ...'*

'You *are such a nuisance,' said the father. Nevertheless, he gave his son a ten rupee note.*

*The child took it to the market and returned with a chocolate. He offered it to his father. 'Today is your birthday, Papa. Happy Birthday!!!'*

*The father was thrilled.*

Now, what did the son do? The money with which he purchased the chocolate was not his; he had taken it from his father. The father could as well have gone to the market himself and purchased the chocolate. But in giving the chocolate to his father, the child expressed his love.

Similarly, all we have belongs to the Lord in the first place; the whole world is His. **But by serving him with our body, mind,**

**and wealth, we express our love for Him. Such loving service is the heart of devotion and endears us to the Lord.**

In endless lives, we remained beggars before Him. Now we must stop it and, as an expression of our true love, learn to give to Him instead. When the Lord sees, 'This soul is giving Me his all and wants nothing from Me', the Lord also offers His all. In fact, He goes to the extent of becoming a servant of His devotee.

We read in the scriptures that God gets bound by His devotees' love. It is such pure selfless love that binds Him. The Shreemad Bhagavatam states:

*ahaṁ bhakta-parādhīno hy asvatantra iva dvija*
*sādhubhir grasta-hṛidayo bhaktair bhakta-jana-priyaḥ*

(9.4.63)

'I am not independent; I am controlled by My devotees. Since they are devoid of material desires, I reside in the core of their hearts. Even the devotees of My devotees are very dear to Me.'

In conclusion, when we practice pure loving devotion towards the Supreme Divine Personality, then our hearts become clean and truly satisfied. In every interaction, the foremost thought in our mind will be 'Let me act in a way that is pleasing to God.' And then, we simultaneously develop an attitude of loving service in all our social, professional, and familial dealings.

The sequence of the last six chapters was designed to help us grasp, in a step-by-step manner, the wisdom we need for awakening our best self. The next topic is placed at the end, but it is so important it is required throughout the entire journey to manifest our best self.

## Key Takeaways

- For a happy and successful life, we are required to adroitly navigate a variety of social and familial connections with positivity and maturity.
- Expectations ruin relationships. We want others to act in certain ways, and when they do not, we become upset.
- True love is that where our goal in a relationship is to serve and give happiness to the other.
- The foundation of true love is a service attitude—the desire to benefit the other, without seeking any reward in return.
- For developing a service attitude, we must first perfect our love for God.
- Most people do business in the name of bhakti. True devotion is that where we only seek the pleasure of God.
- God becomes enslaved by those devotees who love Him selflessly, and He gives them His all.

# 7
# The Law of Mentorship

WHETHER IN professional work or in spiritual growth, results depend not just on hard work but also on smart work. This is where mentors become invaluable. We receive proper guidance from them, which is not otherwise readily accessible. Good mentors can save us from countless mistakes and years of fumbling in the dark.

Sir Isaac Newton realized that mentors extended his vision and enabled him to attain greater heights. He said: 'If I have seen further than others, it is by standing upon the shoulders of giants.'

Let me share with you some interesting data about mentoring.

- Employees who received mentoring were promoted five times more often than those who did not have mentors.
  Source: Gartner 2006.

- Seventy-one per cent of Fortune 500 corporations invest in mentoring programmes because they feel it is worthwhile.
  Source: Centre for Workplace Leadership 2016.
- Seventy-five per cent of executives, when asked about what played a key role in their careers, pointed to mentoring.
  Source: American Society for Training and Development.
- Ninety-five per cent of mentees said the experience motivated them to do their absolute best.
  Source: *The War for Talent* by Ed Michaels, Helen Handfield-Jones, and Beth Axelrod.
- Eighty-four per cent of mentees said mentors helped them avoid costly mistakes.
  Source: *Harvard Business Review* 2015.

In the modern world, the value of mentoring is increasingly being appreciated. Therefore, it is worthwhile to understand this topic in depth, both for personal development and professional success.

## Who Is a Mentor?

The word 'mentor' is a Greek word meaning a wise and trusted advisor. In the epic Odyssey, Mentor was a loyal and trusted advisor to King Odysseus. While the king was away, Mentor became the teacher of Prince Telemachus, building a relationship of trust and affection, as a coach, counsellor, and protector.

In due course, the word became popular around the world. Similar words have been used in various cultures and languages around the world. I am sharing below a few for you to savour.

**In Greek, the word 'mentor' came to mean a wise person, who was also a trusted advisor, friend, and teacher.**

**Among the Japanese and Chinese**, the designation 'sensei' is used as an honorific term for a martial arts teacher. The word literally means 'the one who came before'.

**In Tibet**, a 'lama' is a kind and compassionate teacher of dhamma (dharma), the path to enlightenment. The Dalai Lama is the 'highest ranking teacher' in Tibetan Buddhism.

**The Italians** have the word 'maestro' to designate a teacher of music. It is short form for maestro di cappella, meaning master of the chapel.

**The French** use the word 'tutor' to refer to a private teacher, trainer, and well-wisher.

**The English** word 'guide' is self-descriptive. It is used for one who knows the way and shows the way. The word denotes the ability to see and point out the better path.

**In America**, the word gaining popularity is 'coach'. Four hundred years ago, coach referred to a horse-drawn carriage that was used to carry people from one place to another. Now, the word is used for a personal teacher and trainer who takes us forward in life.

**In India**, since thousands of years, the word 'guru' is used for a person of great knowledge, wisdom, and authority, who guides others. The *Advayatāraka Upaniṣhad* states:

> *guśhabdastvandhakāraḥ syāt ruśhabdastannirodhakaḥ*
> *andhakāranirodhitvāt gururityabhidhīyate* (verse 16)

'The syllable *gu* means darkness, and the syllable *ru*, to dispel it. Hence, one who dispels our darkness and brings us into the light of knowledge is the guru.'

**In Sanskrit**, the word 'guru' also connotes 'one who is heavy', or profound due to his depth of knowledge.

## The Need for Mentors

Whether it is professional career, sports accomplishments, musical excellence, or in any other field of human endeavour, the benefits of mentors are invaluable. Here are some of the widely acknowledged reasons why we need mentors:

1. ***Mentors provide us with distilled and reliable knowledge from the richness of their personal experience.*** By ourselves, we would have had to struggle for decades, learning from failures and successes. But with help from mentors, we get easy access to invaluable wisdom without the accompanying labour.
2. ***Mentors are role models.*** The army generals know the importance of role models. Stories of their heroic feats are the fodder that inspires others to emulate them. Modelling is widely used as a powerful way to develop skills, personality, and character.
3. ***Mentors provide personal coaching.*** They can assess our strengths and weaknesses, and as a result, point out the areas where we need improvement. Filmmaker George Lucas noted, 'Mentors have a way of seeing more of our faults than we would like. It's the only way we grow.'
4. ***Mentors provide encouragement and hope.*** The path to accomplishment is never easy, and left to us, we could easily succumb to obstacles. But if we receive moral backing and cheerleading from an expert, that becomes our support system. Mentors enable us to hope for success and see the light at the end of the tunnel.
5. ***Mentors are disciplinarians.*** They help us observe boundaries that we cannot set for ourselves. Saint Kabir had stated:

*guru kumhāra śhiṣha kumbha hai,*
*gaṛhi gaṛhi kāṛhai khoṭa*
*antara hātha sahāra dai,*
*bāhara bāhai choṭa*

'The guru is akin to a potter, while a student is like a mud vessel. To help the disciple overcome defects, the guru offers harsh advice externally but, like the potter, he gently supports from within.'

6. ***Mentors help us set measurable goals.*** They do not let us become complacent with previous achievements. They challenge us to keep raising our bar for ever greater life successes.

Time to state the seventh divine law:

## The Law of Mentorship

*Having a good mentor in any field helps us set goals, shorten the learning curve, receive encouragement, stay focused, avoid pitfalls, and much more.*

To look for a mentor is not a sign of weakness; on the contrary, it shows you are intelligent enough and motivated enough to succeed on the path. The American correspondent, John Crosby, summed it up well, 'Mentoring is a brain to pick, an ear to listen, and a push in the right direction.'

## Qualities of a Good Mentor

Just because mentors bestow immense benefits does not mean we should simply rush in to make anyone and everyone a mentor. I am reminded of an anecdote.

*Two tramps were sitting side-by-side on a bench in a park. Their clothes were tattered, faces unkempt, shoes worn out, and stomachs empty.*

*The first tramp asked the second, 'What is the reason why you failed so miserably in life?'*

*The second replied, 'I did not listen to good advice from anyone.' He then asked the first, 'What is the cause of your dereliction?'*

*The first tramp responded, 'I listened to everyone's advice.'*

Both sides are dangerous—having too many advisors or not having any. Hence, there is a popular saying in Hindi: *pānī piyo chhāna ke, guru banāo jāna ke* 'Drink water only after filtering; make a guru only after assessing.'

Here are some traits we must look for in mentors:

1. ***A good mentor is an expert.*** This is straightforward logic. If you wish to learn music, you approach expert musicians to study under them. If you desire to learn art, you find good artists to coach you. Similarly, mentors can only be helpful if they possess reliable and expert knowledge, which has matured to wisdom with experience.
2. ***A good mentor leads by example.*** We tend to become like the people we admire deeply. Consequently, our counsellor should be the role model we are inspired to emulate. Thus,

we should see in our personal tutor, the knowledge, skills, and character worthy of emulation.

3. ***A helpful mentor is one who is available.*** Personal advice and counselling require access to our tutor. For example, suppose you are entering the corporate world, and hope to become mentee of someone senior in the organization. Now, most knowledgeable in the field would be the company's CEO. But if you have no access to him, what purpose would it serve?
4. ***A trustworthy mentor has proven experience.*** As the Chinese proverb says: 'To know the way, ask those who are coming back.' Since the mentor has been there and done that, we can trust his advice and knowledge.
5. ***A good mentor provides friendship and support.*** In marketing, research shows that the most effective salespeople are those who do not try to sell their wares; instead, they help customers solve their problems through the goods they sell. Customers are able to sense who is trustworthy and who isn't. 'This person can be trusted', they sense. 'He or she is not here to fulfil a personal agenda.'

Similarly, while seeking help from mentors, the question paramount in our mind is, 'Do you care for me?' We must see in our teacher that quality of loving care and compassion.

So far, we have discussed the qualities to look for while finding suitable mentors in any field. Now, let us go deeper into the topic of mentors in spiritual science, since the purpose of this book is to help our inner growth.

## Need for a Spiritual Mentor

We saw the numerous benefits of having mentors in material pursuits. For spiritual progress, a mentor is even more advantageous. Such a mentor is known as 'guru'. The scriptures and saints go to the extent of declaring the guru as indispensable for awakening our best self.

Jagadguru Shankaracharya stated:

*yāvat gururna kartavyo tāvanmuktirna labhyate*
*tasmāt guruśhcha kartavyo guruṁ binā na siddhyati*

'Unless one takes shelter of a guru, one cannot attain salvation. Hence, surrender to a guru, without whom you cannot achieve perfection.'

Similarly, Saint Kabir had said:

*rāma rahe bana bhītare guru kī pūjā nā āsa*
*rahe kabīra pākhaṇḍa saba, jhūṭhe sadā nirāśha*

'For those who say they do not need a guru because God is in the forest and elsewhere, Saint Kabir says that such people are hypocrites, and they are always disappointed.'

Why do these saints emphasise the need for a guru? The Vedic scriptures inform us that all souls in the material realm are suffering from an affliction. That disease is not physical, but spiritual. Its name is *agyān*, or nescience. The Ramayan states:

*moha sakala vyādhina kara mūlā*

'Ignorance is the root cause of all our problems.'

We do try to dispel it. We school ourselves, we get educational degrees and qualifications, but from the spiritual perspective, ignorance persists because despite our academic attainments, the anger, greed, and pride remain within us.

*A few decades ago, a sociologist from Europe went to Congo in Africa to research aboriginal tribes. His studies brought him in touch with a community of cannibals in the forest. He was astonished to know that the headman's son had been on scholarship to Oxford for graduation.*

*'You are college-educated, and yet you practice cannibalism?' the sociologist asked the youth. 'What difference did college education make to you?'*

*'Well, the difference is this. First, I was eating human flesh with my fingers, and now I eat it with a knife and fork.'*

Now, that is only a joke. But the point is that formal education does not suffice in removing the ignorance within us. So, how can we dispel the spiritual nescience covering us since endless lifetimes?

The Shreemad Bhagavatam states:

*anādy-avidyā-yuktasya puruṣhasyātma-vedanam*
*svato na sambhavād anyas tattva-jño jñāna-do bhavet*

(11.22.10)

In this verse, Lord Krishna explains to Uddhav that since endless lifetimes the intellect of the souls is covered by ignorance. This cannot go by self-analysis; there is need for receiving knowledge from a guru, who is a knower of the Absolute Truth.

If mere thinking was sufficient to gain knowledge, then the cowherd boy in the story below would not have gotten into so much trouble.

*A simple farmer boy would milk his cow every morning. During the day, the cow would leisurely graze in the farm pasture. The bovine's horns were an oddity. They were bent inwards—almost touching each other—thereby creating a roundish space between them and the top of the head.*

*While milking her, the cowherd boy would daily wonder, 'Can my head fit into this gap or not?'*

*One-and-a-half years went by. Finally, his curiosity got the better of him. He held the horns of the cow and tried inserting his head into the gap. The head did go through, but as a result, the cow was startled. It straightened its neck, thereby lifting its head.*

*Now, the farm boy's feet lifted off the ground. To counter the pressure coming on him, he put his arms around the cow's neck. This scared the cow even further. It began mooing loudly, jumping with its hind legs. The boy realized he would get strangulated; he screamed for help.*

*Hearing his frantic pleas, some villagers came running to the rescue. They grabbed the cow and released the boy. Surprised at how he had gotten entangled, they questioned him, 'One should think before doing anything. Did you not deliberate before doing such a foolish thing?'*

*'Who said I did not think?' retorted the boy. 'I was contemplating over it for one-and-a-half years before I put my head in there.'*

When the cowherd boy's thinking itself was defective, no matter how long he thought, it did not solve the problem. Similarly, in the previous verse, Ved Vyas states that under the influence of maya—our intellect is also afflicted with five defects. What are they? The *Yoga Sutras* call them *pañchakleśh*.

*avidyāsmitā raga dveṣhābhiniveśhāḥ kleśhāḥ*

(*Sādhanā Pāda* 2.3)

'The five *kleśhas* afflicting us are: *avidyā*, *asmitā*, *rāg*, *dveṣh,* and *abhiniveśh*.'

Let us understand them briefly for our purpose:

***Avidyā***: This is the nescience due to which we have forgotten our divine spiritual nature. Instead, we look upon ourselves as the body made of matter.

***Asmitā***: This refers to the ego. It is our false sense of self-identity arising from identification with our possessions, designations, education, and so on.

***Rāg***: It is the attachment of our mind to objects and persons, which has distorted our understanding.

***Dveṣh***: This is the negative attachment or resentment. The intellect again gets distorted by it.

***Abhiniveśh***: The idea of death makes us paranoid, since we do not realize our soul is eternal. The apprehension of ceasing to exist forever naturally affects our values and perceptions.

The *Yoga Sutras* state that our intellect is warped by these five afflictions. Thus, no matter how hard and long we contemplate, we cannot free ourselves from nescience. Hence, all the Vedic scriptures declare in unison that divine knowledge must be received from a guru.

The *Chhāndogya Upaniṣhad* states: *āchāryavān puruṣho veda* (6.14.2) 'Only through a guru can you understand the Vedas.' The *Pañchadaśhī* continues:

> *tatpādāmburu hadvandva sevā nirmala chetasām*
> *sukhabodhāya tattvasya viveko 'yaṁ vidhīyate* (1.2)

'Serve the guru with a pure mind, giving up doubts. He will then bring you great happiness by bestowing scriptural knowledge and discrimination.'

The Bhagavad Gita goes on:

*tad viddhi praṇipātena paripraśhnena sevayā*
*upadekṣhyanti te jñānaṁ jñāninas tattva-darśhinaḥ* (4.34)

**'Learn the Truth by approaching a spiritual master. Enquire from him with reverence and render service unto him. Such an enlightened saint can impart knowledge unto you because he has seen the Truth.'**

An interesting confirmation of this principle comes from the divine *leelas* of Lord Ram during His descension on earth. Even He went to a spiritual preceptor for knowledge. As God, He was omniscient; He did not need a guru's support for acquiring knowledge, yet He wished to establish a precedent for us to emulate. To teach us that we will need the guidance of a guru, Lord Ram Himself received instruction at the feet of Guru Vasishth.

Again, Lord Krishna did the same thing. He went to Sandipani Muni's *gurukul* in Ujjain, and there, He learned sixty-four sciences in sixty-four days. How did He complete His education so quickly? The reason was that He did not actually any require any study; He was merely enacting a pastime that would set an example for humankind.

We have understood in various ways, through logic, life-examples, and scriptural testimony, the need for a guru to successfully awaken our best self. The next logical question is: how can we find such a guru?

## Finding a Genuine Guru

It is not difficult for people to understand the need for a guru. In India, the idea gets ingrained from childhood itself. More important is the question, how can we know if someone is a true guru? Unfortunately, very few people know the answer to this question. And that is why there are so many imposters in society duping innocent people.

Consequently, we discuss below some points for recognizing a genuine saint. Let me first explain the safeguards while searching for a guru.

***Precautions***

Firstly, **external appearance and attire should never be the criteria for judging a saint.** Else anyone can don the ochre garb and pretend to be a holy person. *mana na raṅgāe ho raṅgāe jogī kapaṛā* Saint Kabir said, 'Look! The yogi has not coloured his mind; he has only coloured his clothes.' For our purpose, we need to find a yogi whose heart is coloured in love for God.

Now, the second precaution. **Genuine saints do not dupe people by pretending to give material boons.** Nowadays many imposters run a business of offering false blessings. People approach them with worldly desires and these fake saints play a game of chance. They offer baseless boons some of which come true by sheer chance. Those whose desires are fulfilled think it was by the blessing they received, and they do propaganda of the imposter amongst others, 'Go to this baba and by his blessings your wishes will be fulfilled.' This is how phony babas become popular.

True saints are those who have realized the illusory nature of worldly pleasures. Hence, they want their followers to be enriched with spiritual treasures and not blindly run after material opulence.

Now, the third safeguard. **True saints do not try to win over people by performing cheap miracles.** Not knowing any better, society gets tremendously impressed by supernatural acts. A phrase common amongst people is: *chamatkāra ko namaskāra hai*. 'We salute the miracles.' However, these sensational acts are displayed by virtue of three kinds of siddhis:

- **Tamasic siddhi.** In it, the baba worships ghosts and spirits, and enlists their help to do things that impress others.
- **Rajasic siddhi.** In it, an ascetic, by the performance of austerities, develops the ability to somewhat improve people's health, business, etc. The benefit is temporary, because ultimately everyone is under the Law of Karma and gets the results of their own actions.
- **Sattvic siddhi.** By virtue of yogic sadhana, one develops various supernatural abilities some of which include levitating on water, knowing another's thoughts, and manifesting objects. However, these are all material powers, which cannot provide the divine wealth our soul is seeking.

These three kinds of siddhis are not the criteria for finding a true saint. **The real siddhi we should see in saints is the amazing spiritual miracle of transforming people.** A popular Hindi couplet states:

*pārasa meṅ aura santoṅ meṅ, bahuta antaro jāna*
*vaha lohā kāñchana kare, vaha kare āpu samāna*

'A *pāras* (philosopher's stone) can only convert iron into gold but not into another *pāras*. However, saints have the mystical ability to transform worldly people into saints like themselves.' This is the real miracle we wish to see, not just some cheap gimmick, such as the ability to manifest a gold chain.

We have discussed the safeguards in recognizing saints. Let us now come to the signs by which they can be known.

## Recognizing a True Saint

The *Muṇḍak Upaniṣhad* of the *Atharva Veda* informs us of the qualities of a guru. It states:

*tadvijñānārthaṁ sagurumevābhigachchhet*
*samitpāṇiḥ śhrotriyaṃ brahmaniṣhṭham* (1.2.12)

'To realize the Absolute Truth, approach with faith a guru who is both *śhrotriya* and *brahmaniṣhṭh*.'

In this mantra, two qualifications are mentioned for a guru: 1) the guru should be *śhrotriya*, meaning 'knower of the scriptures', and 2) the guru should be *brahmaniṣhṭh*, meaning 'situated on the level of God-realization'.

In other words, the guru should be both theoretically erudite and practically realized. Accordingly, let us now understand what we must look for in a guru.

The first point is that the guru should possess the theoretical knowledge of the scriptures. We should recognize him as an expert in scriptural texts. On this point, it is necessary to qualify that there have been saints in history who were illiterate, and as a result, naturally not well-versed in the sacred books. Dhanna Jat, Sadhna Kasai, and Choka Mela are some such popular saints. Yet, by their past *sanskārs* and God's grace, they attained the supreme goal.

However, from the seeker's point of view, it is best to find a guru who is scholarly. The reason is that if a saint tenders lay explanations without reference to the scriptures, then we will not easily get convinced. But if the saint is erudite the holy books and can teach us truths based on them, then we will quickly gain faith and develop firm resolve. Hence, **the first point to check is that the guru should be an expert in the theoretical knowledge of the scriptures.**

Let us now come to **the second point. The guru must have practically realized the Truth.** This is particularly important, as only one who has attained the Truth can help us do the same. Consider the following story.

*One man reached a river's edge, where a motley crowd was sitting under a tree. This man needed to wade across since there were no boats around. But having no knowledge about this watercourse, he was unsure about what would be the best point for crossing it. So, he asked the people sitting around, 'Sirs, can you please tell me from where I should cross this river?'*

*Among them was a blind man. He immediately spoke up, 'Do not hesitate any further. You are at the perfect spot. Just walk into the stream and you will be on the other side in a jiffy.'*

*Hearing him, this man thought to himself, 'He cannot see and has never crossed the river by himself. Of what use is his advice?'*

*In the meantime, a lame person spoke up, 'No, I will tell you a better route. Walk up fifty steps and cross from there.'*

*The man again thought to himself, 'This person is lame. He could never have crossed the stream by himself either. Why should I believe him?'*

*Then a third person began to speak. In measured words, he said, 'Sir, do not worry. I live in a village on the other side. Every morning I come across the river and then return in the evening. All you need to do is to walk 400 meters upstream until you come to a banyan tree. Step into the stream there and keep walking but ensure that the current does not let you drift downstream. You will be on the highest line of the riverbed and will have no problem reaching the other side.'*

*Now, the man thought, 'This person is experienced. He has probably been doing it for many years. His knowledge is trustworthy. Let me try it out.'*

Similarly, we want a guru who has practical experience of the spiritual journey. It means, he followed the spiritual process, purified the mind and intellect, received divine grace by surrendering to God, and then got practical realization of the Absolute Truth. It is in such a guru that we can repose our faith.

Lord Krishna referred to such a saint as *tattva darśhi* (one who is a seer of the Truth). He said to Arjun: 'An enlightened Saint can impart knowledge unto you because he has seen the Truth.' (4.34) We want to find such a seer of the Truth.

Point number three. If a saint is a *tattva darśhi,* you will find another symptom in such a person. **Such a guru has the capability to resolve our doubts related to spiritual sadhana.** In contrast, merely theoretical pandits, who are without practical realization, do not possess this ability. Simply studying the scriptures without implementing the teachings only leads to further confusion. The Mahabharat states:

*śhrutir vibhinnā smṛitayo vibhinnāḥ*
*naiko muniryasya vachaḥ pramāṇam*

'There are so many scriptures in the form of *śhrutis* and *smṛitis*, with each disserting mutually contradictory principles. Even big scholars become baffled on reading them.'

The Ramayan states the same thing:

*śhruti purāna bahu kaheu upāī,*
*chhūṭa na adhika adhika arujhāī*

'The *śhrutis* and *smṛitis* teach many techniques. Merely acquiring theoretical knowledge of them does not lead to clarity, rather, it increases the confusion.'

These scriptures are divine and profound; their import is beyond our finite material intellect. This is why they should be studied under the guidance of a guru. Realized saints have practical experience of the spiritual path and the supreme goal. Therefore, they can easily resolve the aspirants' doubts and help them develop clarity of understanding.

The fourth point is that the saint's words are immensely powerful because they are not just learned from a book; they are spoken from the depths of realization. It is one thing to hear a theoretical pandit expound on some principle, and quite another to hear the same precept from the mouth of a genuine guru. We may have read the same bit of knowledge in books many times over—that we are not the body but spirit souls—but not been impacted by it. Yet **when we hear the same message from a saint's mouth, it goes deep into our hearts and transforms us forever. That is the power of a God-realized saint's *vāṇī* (speech).**

The Bible states: 'The holy men of God spoke as they were moved by the holy ghost.' (2 Peter 1:21) Truly, since the saints are surrendered to the Lord, they become His mediums in the work of spiritual welfare. It is as if God speaks through them.

Now, we come to the fifth and most important point for recognizing a guru. **When we associate with genuine saints, by the power of their satsang, we naturally develop detachment from mundane worldly things and attachment to divine matters.**

Compare this to the properties of fire.

*Let us say, you are in the open on a winter night, and are shivering in the cold. Thirty yards away, there is a fire burning, and its heat is not reaching you. But, as you walk closer to the fire, with every step you take towards it, the heat grows in your body and the cold reduces.*

Similarly, true saints are like fireballs of God-consciousness. It cannot happen that we associate with them, and we do not experience detachment from the mundane or attachment to the divine. This experience of their transformational power upon us is the *pratyakṣh pramāṇ* (practical evidence) of a saint.

However, a disclaimer is required for this point. The impact of a genuine saint varies from person to person. Take the example of a magnet. Its nature is to attract iron. Do the following experiment with it.

*Put five needles of different compositions around a magnet. The first needle is of pure iron. In the second needle, iron has been alloyed with a trace of copper. The third needle has iron and copper in a ratio of fifty-fifty. The fourth contains mainly copper and a trace of iron, while the fifth needle is of pure copper.*

*Put these needles around the magnet. What will happen? The pure iron needle will be speedily attracted. The needles alloyed with copper will experience a lesser pull. And the needle with no iron will not get pulled, even if you tie it to the magnet.*

True saints are like the magnet, and our souls are like the needles. On meeting saints, those whose heart is pure are immediately attracted. But the extent to which our heart is impure, to that extent the saint's impact gets impeded.

That is why we read in the biographies of saints that a group of people went to meet a saint. One saw him and immediately did an about turn from the world. The other had darshan of the saint but did not do an about turn, he or she did a left turn or a right turn. The third met the saint but remained unaffected. The fourth hurled abuses upon the saint and returned.

Why is there a difference? Sri Ramakrishna Paramahansa expressed it so aptly: 'As a nail cannot enter into stone, but can easily be driven into the earth, so the advice of the pious does not affect the soul of a worldly man, while it enters deep into the heart of a believer.'

**Those whose hearts are pure experience such a pull on meeting a true saint, that they immediately feel inspired, 'This is the person I was searching for', their hearts seem to announce.** But those whose hearts are impure keep fluctuating between faith and doubt. 'He is a saint. No, he is just a worldly person. No, there is something special about him. Well, actually, there is nothing special.' Like a pendulum, they move forward and backward in their own place.

Now, this phenomenon complicates our problem of finding genuine saints. Let us say we have been associating with a baba for twenty years and have not experienced any spiritual benefit—neither attachment to God nor detachment from the mundane. Then what should we conclude? Is the baba not a true saint as we thought he was? Or is our heart so impure that he could not impact us?

The answer to the dilemma is to associate with several saints. Quietly go and sit in their satsang, lectures, kirtans, etc. You do not need to argue or quarrel. Simply observe their impact upon yourself. **Are you developing *anurāg* (love) towards God; are**

**you growing in *vairāgya* (detachment) from the world? The saint who creates the deepest spiritual impact is the one you are looking for.** If you use this formula, you will not get cheated, because you are using *pratyakṣh pramāṇ*, direct observable evidence.

Equipped with this safeguard and ways to find true saints we can now embark upon it.

## Finding Our Spiritual Mentor

If we had come under the guidance of a God-realized saint in our past life but could not complete our journey, in the present life, the Lord will directly put us in touch with another saint, so that we may continue forward. But if in previous lives, we had not reached that point of spiritual evolution, then in the present birth we will have to search.

While searching, it is possible we took shelter under a guru but later realized that this person was not a genuine saint. In that case, we should not hesitate to quietly become neutral and move on. It is just like when you go a doctor for a physical cure. If you do not derive benefit, you do not think that whether you live or die, you cannot change your doctor. Nor do you waste time fighting with the doctor; you simply move on.

But in the case of gurus, we often hear people saying, 'I have made a guru once. Now whether he takes me to heaven or hell, I am stuck with this guru for life.' Well, the fact is that in our previous life we had a different guru, and in the life before we had a different one. We may not realize it, but we have already changed so many gurus in innumerable births. So, in this life as well, we have the right to keep searching until we find the proper personality. **Once we do reach the feet of a true saint, then we should stop all the search, and start the process of practical sadhana under him.** Any further searches would be a distraction and waste of time.

While finding your guru, do keep in mind that the guru's teachings should be in accordance with your *sanskārs*. Even genuine saints have very dissimilar teachings. One propagates the path of *Ashtang Yog*, another recommends devotion and surrender, while a third asks us to simply focus upon self-knowledge.

People often ask, 'Why is it that even among genuine saints there are such differing teachings?' The answer is that God arranges for teachers at all levels because students are at different levels. Just as in schools, there is need for primary-school teachers, middle-school teachers, and high-school teachers.

Sometimes a teacher may be a PhD but, when assigned to a primary class, she may teach 2 + 2 = 4. This does not imply that the teacher only knows so much. What she is teaching is determined not by the level of her knowledge but by the limits of how much the students can understand.

Similarly, all true saints do the work God has assigned to them, and they all are equally praiseworthy. If they are genuine saints, we should never criticize their works. Instead, **we should look for a teacher who teaches a path that suits our *sanskārs*.**

Now comes the final point regarding finding a saint. God is seated in our hearts and knows our innermost desires. He leads us to our guru when He sees that we have developed aspiration for achieving spiritual growth. Further, God inspires us with the faith that we may surrender to the guru and benefit from him.

Jagadguru Kripaluji Maharaj explained this so beautifully:

*hari kṛipā guru mile, govinda rādhey*
*guru kṛipā hari mile, saba ko batā de*

(*Radha Govind Geet*)

'First God will grace you and help you find the guru. Then, the guru will grace you and help you reach God.' So, **we will get connected to a true guru by the grace of the Lord when our longing for spiritual growth is intense enough.** However, to attract the divine grace, we must also put in the effort to search.

In the past few sections, I have explained the *Guru Tattva*. Sometimes people request, 'Swamiji, please tell us who is a true guru in present times?' I explain that you must search and reach your own conclusions. Only then will you develop a firm and unshakeable bond with any guru you make. Hence, my task here is simply to help you understand the theoretical principles related to the Law of Mentorship and the topic of guru. After that, it is for you to find your true guru.

Finally, what should we do if we have not yet found a genuine guru? Should we wait for that day to come? No, we should not wait for a guru; we must immediately begin on the path with full earnest. In the future, as we become eligible for divine grace, we will be led to our spiritual teacher. But until then, we should begin the journey with whatever knowledge we have garnered from saints and scriptures.

Later, when we do come in touch with our guru, he will help us complete the spiritual evolution of our soul to the ultimate destination. Until then, I hope you will find the knowledge in this book helpful for your spiritual progress.

This book was written with the desire to serve you by offering the knowledge of the divine laws of the Universe. If it helps you to take even one step to awaken your best self, I will consider my humble and insignificant effort a success.

## Key Takeaways

- A mentor is a wise person, who is also a trusted advisor, friend, and teacher.
- Good mentors can save us from countless mistakes and years of fumbling in darkness.
- A good mentor should be an expert in the field and a worthy example for us to emulate. The trustworthy mentor should have proven experience and should provide us support and friendship.
- In spirituality, a mentor is indispensable because of the ignorance covering our intellect since endless lifetimes. The spiritual mentor is called 'guru'.
- We should not get conned by imposter gurus who show cheap miracles or pretend to give material boons.
- A genuine guru should be both theoretically erudite and practically realized.
- When we associate with genuine saints, by the power of their satsang, we naturally develop detachment from worldly things and attachment to divine matters.
- God is seated in our hearts. He leads us to our guru when He sees that our aspiration for achieving spiritual growth is intense.

# The Divine Laws Summarized

WE SEE in nature around us, carbon incubated in the earth over billions of years evolving into diamonds. However, the primary purpose of Creation is far greater; it is to nurture the evolution of souls to super-consciousness over a continuum of lifetimes.

Consequently, our soul nudges us to strive ever forward to awaken our best self. The impediment in our inner unfoldment is created by our own lack of awareness of the laws of the Universe.

Like the laws regulating physical phenomena, there are also spiritual principles governing the journey of life. Knowledge of them helps us understand why success comes so easily to some but remains a struggle for others. What are these laws?

The first is the **Law of Infinite Potential.** It helps us realize the glorious destiny of the soul and the infinity of possibilities for our personal growth. It states that **all souls have infinite potential for growth, whatever be their present state.**

This law helps us conclude that the purpose of our human life is to grow. We now want to understand the nature of the journey to that goal. For this, the second law, **The Law of Incremental Growth** becomes useful. It instils in us that **personal excellence and life mastery can only be achieved by consistent small steps of incremental improvement.**

This law emphasizes the importance of repeatedly making better choices with self-discipline. But since willpower is limited, the third divine law teaches us how to tap into a something even more powerful through **The Law of Beliefs.** It explains that **the trajectory of our life is determined by the beliefs we hold in our intellect.**

The biggest force within our personality comes from the beliefs we hold. Among them, the most important belief is our conviction regarding happiness. The paradox is that everyone is running for happiness but begetting suffering instead. Hence, the fourth divine law, **The Law of Happiness**, explains that we are looking for happiness in the wrong place. **True happiness comes by growing from within to become a better person.**

To become better, we must overcome our lower nature, consisting of unwholesome desires, attachments, greed, pride, envy, and aversions. Suppression has the reverse results. Thus, we need to know the fifth divine law, which is **The Law of Sublimation**. It provides the way to conquer our lower impulses. It states that **the sovereign recipe for purifying the mind and its thoughts is to dovetail them towards the Supreme through bhakti.**

Devotion to God sublimates our desires and attachments and makes them divine. The problem is that presently, in the name of devotion, we do business with God. Hence, the sixth divine law, **The Law of Love**, explains the difference between love, lust, and business. It clarifies that **our hearts can only be satisfied by true love, which is a deep and noble affection for the other's happiness, without seeking personal benefit in return.** The basis of this divine love is the service attitude, which must first be developed towards God, and then to all creation.

These six laws have been sequentially numbered to help us grasp, in a step-by-step manner, the wisdom we need for awakening our best self. The seventh and final law, **The Law of Mentorship** is placed at the end, but it is so important that it is required from the beginning to the end of the journey. It says that **having a good mentor in any field helps us shorten the learning curve, set goals, receive encouragement, stay focused, avoid pitfalls, and so much more.** In the spiritual field, the mentor is called 'guru'.

When we come in touch with our guru, he will help us complete the spiritual evolution of our soul to the ultimate destination. Until then, I hope that the knowledge in this book will be helpful for your spiritual progress.

# Glossary

Abhiniveśha – fear of death

Agyān – ignorance

Anurāg – love or positive/favourable attachment

Apauruṣheya – not created by a human

Asmitā – ego

Avidyā – ignorance

Dānī – donor, charity giver

Dveṣha – negative attachment or hatred

Kām – lust. The Vedas define lust as selfishness or self-seeking nature

Mānas rog – mental afflictions such as anger, greed, envy, lust, pride, etc.

Niṣhkām bhakti – worship with the aim of serving God for His happiness alone

Pañchakleśha – five defects of the intellect

Pratyakṣh pramāṇ – directly observable evidence

Prem – true love that is all about giving to the other

Rāga – attachment

Rajo guna – mode of passion

Sadhana – spiritual practice

Sakām bhakti – worship with the aim of fulfilment of material desire

Sanskars – tendencies from past lives

Satsang – association that takes our mind to the Absolute Truth

Sattva guna – mode of goodness

Shraddha – strong belief or faith

Shrutis – the four Vedas

Siddhi – a state of enlightenment or perfection

Smṛitis – 18 Puranas and the two historical texts of Ramayan and Mahabharat

Tamo guna – mode of ignorance

Tattva darśhi – seer of truth; one who has seen/experienced Absolute Truth

Vairāgya – detachment

Vāṇī – speech

Viparyaya – reversal of intellect leading to opposite or incorrect knowledge

Vyāpār – transaction with one party receiving and the other giving

# Index

bhakti, primal form of, 101
Bhartrihari, Saint, 22, 67
*bhrama* (illusion), 61
big momentum, (Big Mo), 37
binge eating, 42
bondage, 85
Bonsai, 82
*Brahma Purāṇ*, 98
Brahman
 definition of, 5
 existence of, 96
 meaning of, 5
*Bṛihadāraṇyak Upaniṣhad*, 78, 97, 118
Business (*vyāpār*), 120
Business with God, 128–31

Casals, Pablo, 7
Centre for Workplace Leadership, 137
*Chaitanya Charitāmṛit*, 23, 131
cheap miracles, 148, 159
*Chhāndogya Upaniṣhad*, 146
choice, dignity of, 26
Choka Mela, 150
*Civilization and Its Discontents*, 74
cognitive intelligence (IQ), 126
Computer Center Corporation (CCC), 30
consciousness, 2–3, 5, 17, 25, 85, 112–13, 154, 160
Crosby, John, 140

Dalai Lama, 138
*dānī*, 121, 163
*Dāsya bhav* (sentiment of servitude), 106
demonic-natured ones, 67
desire, 74, 76, 87, 94
detrimental material desires, 92
Deussen, Paul, 98
*Devi Lok*, 25
Dhanna Jat, 150
divine bliss, 76–78, 83, 107
divine knowledge, 27
divine laws, xiv-xv
divine love for God, 92
Dubai lottery, 29
*dveṣh*, 145, 163
Dwāpar age, 23

Einstein, Albert, 58
*Elegy Written in a Country Churchyard*, 14
emotional intelligence (EQ), 126
enlightenment, 8, 36, 44, 138, 164
Emerson, Ralph Waldo, xii
eternal relationship with god
 eternal relative, 103, 114
 selfless relative, 103
exercise addiction, 42
existence of God, 95–97
expectations ruin relationships, 116–19
 expectations were genuinely selfless, 117
 relational friction, 116
 self-centred desires, 117
 unfulfilled expectations, 116–17

fixed mindset, 7, 13, 27
 vs. growth mindset, 7–9
flawless source of knowledge. *See* Vedas
Francis, Saint, 124
Frankenstein, 17
Freud, Sigmund, 74

Gates, Bill, 29–31
genuine guru, finding of, 147–50

# Guide to Hindi Pronunciation

| | |
|---|---|
| *a* | as *u* in b*u*t |
| ā | as *a* in f*a*r |
| *i* | as *i* in p*i*n |
| ī | as *i* in mach*i*ne |
| *u* | as *u* in p*u*sh |
| ū | as *o* in m*o*ve |
| *e* | as *a* in ev*a*de |
| *ai* | as *a* in m*a*t; sometimes as *ai* in *ai*sle with the only difference that *a* should be pronounced as *u* in b*u*t, not as *a* in f*a*r |
| *o* | as *o* in g*o* |
| *au* | as *o* in pot, or as *aw* in s*aw* |
| *ṛi* | as *ri* in K*ri*shna |
| *ḥ* | it is a strong aspirate; also lengthens the preceding vowel and occurs only at the end of a word. It is pronounced as a final *h* sound |
| *ṁ* | nasalizes and lengthens the preceding vowel and is pronounced as *n* in the French word Bo*n*. |
| *ka* | as *k* in *k*ite |

*kha* as *kh* in Ec*kh*art

*ga* as *g* in *g*oat

*gha* as *gh* in dig*h*ard

*ṅ* as *n* in fi*n*ger

*cha* as *ch* in *ch*anel

*chha* as *chh* in staun*chh*eart

*ja* as *j* in *j*ar

*jha* as *dgeh* in he*dgeh*og

ñ as *n* in lu*n*ch

*ṭa* as *t* in *t*ub

*ṭha* as *th* in ho*th*ead

*ḍa* as *d* in *d*ivine

*ḍha* as *dh* in re*dh*ead

*ṇa* as *n* in bur*n*t

*ta* as *t* in French word ma*t*ron

*tha* as *th* in e*th*er

*da* as *th* in ei*th*er

*dha* as *dh* in Bud*dh*a

*na* as *n* in *n*o

*pa* as *p* in *p*ink

*pha* as *ph* in u*ph*ill

*ba* as *b* in *b*oy

*bha* as *bh* in a*bh*or

*ma* as *m* in *m*an

*ya* as *y* in *y*es

*ra* as *r* in *r*emember

| | |
|---|---|
| *la* | as *l* in *l*ight |
| *va* | as *v* in *v*ine, as *w* in s*w*an |
| śha | as *sh* in *sh*ape |
| *sa* | as *s* in *s*in |
| *ṣha* | as *sh* in *sh*ow |
| *ha* | as *h* in *h*ut |
| *kṣha* | as *ksh* in frea*ksh*ow |
| *jña* | as *gy* in bi*gy*oung |
| *ṛa* | There is no sign in English to represent the sound ड़. It has been written as *ṛa* but the tip of the tongue quickly flaps down. |
| *ṛha* | There is no sign in English to represent the sound ढ़. It has been written as *ṛha* but the tip of the tongue quickly flaps down. |
| *ṛī* | *as ree in* spr*ee* |

# Other Books by the Author

*7 Mindsets for Success, Happiness, and Fulfilment*

*Bhagavad Gita, The Song of God*

*Essence of Hinduism*

*Science of Healthy Diet*

*Spiritual Dialectics*

*The Science of Mind Management*

*Yoga for Mind, Body, and Soul*

**Books for Children**

*Bal-Mukund Wisdom Book*

*Festivals of India*

*Healthy Body, Healthy Mind: Yoga for Children*

*Inspiring Stories for Children* (set of 4 books)

*Mahabharat*

*My Best Friend Krishna*

*Ramayan*

*Saints of India*

# Let's Connect

If you enjoyed reading this book and would like to connect with Swami Mukundananda, you can reach him through any of the following channels:

Websites: *www.swamimukundananda.org, www.jkyog.org, www.jkyog.in*

YouTube channels: 'Swami Mukundananda' and 'Swami Mukundananda Hindi'

Facebook: 'Swami Mukundananda' and 'Swami Mukundananda Hindi'

Instagram: 'Swami Mukundananda' and 'Swami Mukundananda Hindi'

Pinterest: Swami Mukundananda – JKYog

Twitter: Swami Mukundananda (@Sw_Mukundananda)

LinkedIn: Swami Mukundananda

Podcasts: Apple, Google, SoundCloud, Spotify, Stitcher

JKYog Radio: TuneIn app for iOS (Apple App Store) and Android (Google Play Store)

JKYog App: Available for iOS (Apple App Store) and Android (Google Play Store)

WhatsApp Daily Inspirations: We have two broadcast lists. You are welcome to join either or both.

USA: +1 346-239-9675

India: +91 84489 41008

Email: deskofswamiji@swamimukundananda.org

To bring *7 Divine Laws* or Swami Mukundananda to your organization—as Google, Intel, Oracle, Verizon, United Nations, Stanford University, Yale University, IITs and IIMs have—please write to deskofswamiji@swamimukundananda.org

# About the Author

**Swami Mukundananda** is a world-renowned spiritual teacher and an authority on mind management. He grew up in India and earned his degrees from the prestigious IIT Delhi and IIM Calcutta. Having learned the Vedic scriptures at the feet of Jagadguru Shree Kripaluji Maharaj, he now spends his time explaining the path of true, ever-lasting happiness to people everywhere. In between his hectic schedule, he writes books and commentaries, records CDs and DVDs, and guides a worldwide congregation of devotees.

Swamiji's lectures are humorous, his arguments are logical and well laid-out, and most of all, his advice is practical. His lectures on YouTube and other social media platforms are loved and followed by millions. He is the author of two bestsellers – *7 Mindsets for Success, Happiness, and Fulfilment* and *The Science of Mind Management*. Swamiji divides his time between India and the US.